Let's Get Straight to the Point

Home Inspection 101
for Buyers and Sellers

Douglas Cavalieri

Belmont City Press LLC

Published by **Belmont City Press LLC**

For permission requests, please contact:
Belmont City Press LLC
www.BelmontCityPress.com

Contents

Dedication 1

About Douglas Cavalieri and Arrow Home Inspection 3

What is a Home Inspection? 7

1. Roofing 17
2. What to Know About Chimneys 27
3. Exterior Elements 37
4. Site Elements 49
5. Structural Elements 59
6. Attics and Framing 71
7. Behind the Bathroom Door 81
8. Kitchens 87
9. Interior Elements 95
10. Foundation and Substructure 103
11. Foundation Area Water Penetration 113
12. Heating Systems and Air-Conditioning 121
13. Hot Water 133
14. Plumbing System 141
15. Electrical System 149

16. Asbestos 157

17. Inspection Types & Add-On Services 163

18. Radon 167

19. Sewer Scope Inspections 171

20. Sellers, Get Ahead of the Market 175

Book an Inspection 181

To my mother and father—

Your faith in me built the solid foundation I stand on today. Because you believed in me, I learned to believe in myself. Thank you for encouraging me to chase big dreams and become the man I am. After all, *a house built on rock will not fall.*

To my brother—

My first friend. Thank you for showing me what real perseverance looks like, for teaching me to trust my training, and always look in the direction I want to go.

To every mentor who ever showed me the ropes...

To every tradesperson who reached back and pulled me forward...

To the clients and agents who remind me daily why I love what I do...

Thank you; for the lessons, the laughs, and for helping me build a life and a business that gets straight to the point.

And to Willow, the best girl I ever knew. Who knew that four paws and a wet nose could open so many doors? Your quiet loyalty, steady companionship, and sweet nature have helped me make more friends than I ever expected and reminded me, every day, to enjoy the journey.

About Douglas Cavalieri and Arrow Home Inspection

Every Shingle, Every Nail, Every Lesson

When you meet Doug Cavalieri at your home inspection, you're shaking hands with nearly 30 years of construction knowledge, hard-won experience, and a deep-seated respect for the homes he inspects. But that expertise didn't come from a textbook, it came from hauling shingles at thirteen years old for a neighbor who did wood siding. It came from avoiding the freezing winters, by hanging drywall inside to keep the work going. (Pretty savvy, for a 13-year old). It came from framing houses and installing tile and cabinetry in his teens and early twenties. Every detail Doug learned, every trade he touched, defined a step in the path that eventually led him here; to Arrow Home Inspections.

By the time Doug graduated from Mt. Hope High School in Bristol, Rhode Island, he had already built his first house; literally. As part of his senior-year "Home Building Project," he and a team of upperclassmen built a home from the foundation up. For most students, it was a one-time project. For Doug, it was the start of a lifelong passion.

Out of high school, Doug dove straight into the trades. Roofing, siding, tile work, remodeling, there wasn't a task he wouldn't try or a skill he didn't want to learn. But he wasn't just collecting paychecks. He was studying, observing, and mastering the intricate relationship between the pieces of a house. His particular talent was finish work, those final details that only someone with real vision and patience can get right. He learned to see the whole project and still spot what others missed.

Eventually, Doug joined a framing crew and for years, focused on the bones of the home, the part most people never see but that every aspect of the structure depends on. He loved it. But then, in 2018, the possibly predictable-but-unthinkable happened: a back injury put him on the sidelines. For a man whose hands had always done the talking, it was a turning point. Would he return to physically demanding labor, risking further injury? Or was it time to bring all of his hard-earned skills together under one roof?

Doug chose the latter, a decision that allowed him to use everything he knew, every lesson from every trade, in a way that helped people. He capitalized on an opportunity to become a home inspector.

In 2019, he trained, certified, and went to work for a national firm, conducting over 2,000 home inspections. He was thorough, personable, and most of all, he was trusted. By 2023, he had earned the title of *Home Inspector of the Year*. But Doug isn't one to rest on accolades. That award wasn't the finish line, it was the signpost. In July 2024, driven by a desire to have more control over the types of services offered and a customer service philosophy that got *straight to the point*, Arrow Home Inspections was born.

What Arrow Stands For

Doug built Arrow not just to inspect homes, but to guide people through one of the biggest decisions of their lives. At Arrow, inspection means more than ticking boxes. It means educating buyers, reassuring sellers, and equipping real estate agents with insight they can pass on with confidence.

In reviews and testimonials, clients often say Doug “helped them make the right decision.” Sometimes that meant clients moving forward on the house where they’d raise a family and build a home or clients stepping into the next chapter of life with clarity and peace of mind. Sometimes it meant clients would walk away from something they couldn’t take on. Either way, they didn’t feel pressured; they felt informed.

Doug has a way of explaining things that just makes sense. Maybe it’s because he learned every trade from the ground up. Maybe it’s because he never forgot what it was like to be new to it all. His reports don’t just list issues; they tell the story of the house. They highlight concerns in plain terms and offer context that turns stress into clarity. Most reports are delivered the same day. Why? Because Doug knows what it’s like to wait for an answer when your future is on the line.

That’s where the name *Arrow* comes from. Doug believes in getting *straight to the point* with clear, honest, no-nonsense communication that respects your time, your goals, and your investment.

Why a Home Inspection Matters

A home inspection isn't just a checklist, it's peace of mind. It's the difference between surprise repairs and smart planning. It's a snapshot of a house's condition and a blueprint for next steps. It's not designed to scare people or sell them, it's designed to serve them.

Doug started Arrow so he could do just that; serve. Not a company, not a bottom line but the client. With every inspection, he brings his full background to the table and delivers what people actually need: facts, insight, and a professional who gets straight to the point.

Doug doesn't wear a suit, but he's a professional. He doesn't just inspect homes, he interprets them. When clients hire Arrow Home Inspections, they're not just getting a home inspector. They're getting a craftsman, a contractor, a finisher, a framer, a tiler, and a straight shooter. They're getting every lesson Doug Cavalieri has ever learned, delivered "straight to the point" and that makes all the difference.

What is a Home Inspection?

A Snapshot in Time, A Blueprint for the Future

Let's get stright to the point....A home is never finished. It shifts and grows with each new owner, adapting to the styles, needs, and technologies of its time. The fact that homes endure, some for over a century, is a testament to how they're passed hand to hand, generation to generation, each new occupant making repairs, updates, and decisions that carry the house forward.

That's where a home inspection comes in. It doesn't predict the future. It doesn't guarantee perfection. Instead, a home inspection provides a snapshot in time, a detailed assessment of the home's current condition, on the day it was inspected. It creates a baseline that empowers you to plan your next steps, usually with your Agents' guidance. Whether that means asking for repairs, budgeting for updates, or simply moving forward with peace of mind.

Let's take a moment to talk directly to buyers because if you're preparing to purchase a home, you've probably already heard a lot of opinions about what a home inspection is (and isn't). Unfortunately, some of the most common assumptions can lead to confusion or disappointment if not addressed early. So, what is the role of a home inspection in your home buying journey? And what are some of the biggest misconceptions buyers bring into the process? I'm glad you asked.

Misconception: A House Can "Pass" or "Fail" an Inspection

Reality: Home inspections don't issue grades, they provide information.

There is no such thing as failing a home inspection. A home inspection isn't a test, and the inspector isn't a teacher handing out a report card. Instead, inspectors document what they see, pointing out what's working, what's not, and what might require attention in the future.

Misconception: This house failed the inspection.

Reality: The inspection revealed some items that need attention.

A home inspection is meant to identify issues, not to issue a verdict. Even well-maintained homes can have items that show up on a report—some small, some worth a closer look. The goal isn't perfection; it's clarity. Knowing what's going on with the home helps you decide how to move forward, negotiate repairs, or plan for future maintenance.

Misconception: We need a perfect report to move forward.

Reality: We need to understand the condition and plan accordingly.

It's rare for a home to have zero findings. Instead of chasing a flawless report, focus on understanding the significance of what's discovered. Is it a safety issue? A maintenance task? A deal-breaker, or just a future weekend project? An inspection helps you prioritize and make informed decisions, not walk away in fear.

Misconception: New Homes or "Perfect" Homes Don't Need Inspections

Reality: There is no such thing as a perfect house, only well-maintained or newly-built ones.

New construction homes can have issues just like older homes. Missed connections, incomplete installations, or rushed finishes are more common than you'd think. Likewise, homes that appear pristine may have underlying problems, hidden behind fresh paint or staged furniture.

Misconception: This home is immaculate, no need to check.

Reality: Looks can be deceiving. Let's confirm what's behind the walls.

Shiny surfaces and fresh finishes don't tell the whole story. Behind new countertops or flawless staging, there could be missing insulation, reversed plumbing, or improperly installed systems. An inspection isn't about doubting quality, it's about verifying it, so you're not surprised later. Even a brand-new home deserves a baseline record to track future upkeep and warranty concerns.

Misconception: A Home Inspection is Like an Appraisal

Reality: Inspections and appraisals serve different purposes and different people.

An appraisal estimates the market value of the home for the lender. It ensures the house is worth the loan being requested. An inspection, on the other hand, examines the physical condition of the home for (typically) the buyer; their needs, safety, and budget. (Even FHA appraisals, which consider some condition items, do not substitute for a full inspection).

Appraisals:

- Determine value for the bank
- Usually required by lenders
- May note major safety/code issues

Inspections:

- Assesses condition for the buyer
- Optional, in most states (but highly recommended)
- Identifies a wide range of concerns, from minor to major

Misconception: A Home Inspection Predicts the Future

Reality: An inspection is not a crystal ball, it's a snapshot of one moment in time.

Inspectors can't predict what might break six months from now. The role of an inspector is to observe and report on what is visible and accessible at the time of inspection and report that to you. That's it. It's not that inspectors don't care about what may happen later, it's that they can't report on what they can't see or test.

Misconception: The inspector missed this as it broke six months later!

Reality: It wasn't visible or defective at the time of inspection.

An inspection is limited to what's accessible and functioning on the day it's performed. If something looked and worked fine at the time, there may have been no clues of an underlying issue. Just like a routine physical can't prevent a future illness, a home inspection isn't a guarantee—it's a snapshot, not a forecast.

Misconception: I thought the inspection would tell me everything!

Reality: It tells you everything that was discoverable at that time.

Home inspections are thorough but not all-knowing. Inspectors don't open walls or dismantle systems, and certain components can't be tested during extreme weather or if utilities aren't on. The goal is to give you the clearest possible picture based on what could be seen, reached, and operated on inspection day.

What an Inspection Is: A Blueprint, Not a Judgment

A home inspection is a tool; a map, a checklist, a guide to help you understand what you're buying and how to care for it. Think of it as a starting point. You get to choose how to respond:

* Negotiate for repairs or credits

* Budget for short- and long-term maintenance

* Make informed decisions about your next steps

What it is not: a promise, a guarantee, or a lifelong warranty.

What This Book Will Do for Buyers, Sellers, and Agents

Home inspections are often seen as just another box to check or a way to negotiate but they're much more than that. At Arrow, we believe the inspection is one of the most valuable tools for anyone looking to make an informed, empowered decision.

For Buyers: More Than Just a Hurdle, Inspections as a Tool for Confidence

Yes, inspections are traditionally associated with buyers, and for good reason, they offer a deeper look at the condition of the home, beyond fresh paint or new appliances. But a great inspection isn't about finding problems to walk away from; it's about understanding the home you're about to invest in. Whether you're buying your first home or your fifth, an inspection helps you approach the process with clarity, not guesswork.

Sometimes buyers feel nervous that an inspection will "ruin the deal," but the truth is: knowledge is power. A clear, detailed inspection can save you from unexpected costs down the road, help you prioritize repairs, and give you confidence in your purchase, even if the home isn't perfect (spoiler: no home is).

We focus on giving you the full picture in a way that's digestible, not overwhelming. Our goal isn't to scare or sway, it's to explain what's there, what matters most, and what may need your attention now versus later. In a competitive market, where waiving contingencies is sometimes considered (where allowed), even our simplified Walk & Talk inspections offer peace of mind when time is tight.

In the end, it's not about avoiding issues it's about facing them with insight and strategy. An informed buyer is a confident buyer, and we're here to help you feel just that.

For Sellers: Why Understanding Home Inspections Matters Before You List

If you're planning to sell your home, understanding the role of a home inspection can help you avoid unnecessary surprises and navigate the process with confidence. A home inspection is not just for buyers, it's a valuable tool for sellers, too. Hiring a home inspector to perform a pre-listing inspection gives you insight into how others may view your home and allows you to take proactive steps before your property ever hits the market.

Even if you've had your home maintained over the years or passed a previous inspection during your own purchase, keep in mind: inspections are snapshots taken by different professionals, at different moments in time, and for different audiences. Just because your inspector didn't flag something as a concern years ago doesn't mean a new inspector or a potential buyer won't question it today. Small things like a missing GFCI outlet, a slow drain, or a stain from a long-ago leak might feel minor to you but could raise red flags for someone seeing your home for the first time.

Buyers approach inspections with fresh eyes and their own expectations. What you see as "normal wear and tear" may be interpreted as a future cost or risk by a buyer especially in a competitive market or when emotions are high.

By understanding how inspections work and preparing ahead of time (by doing a pre-listing inspection), you can make informed decisions about repairs, pricing, and how to present your home honestly and effectively. The goal isn't to make the house "perfect." It's to build trust, reduce friction, and make it easy for the next owner to say yes.

For Agents: Guiding, Not Negotiating, the Inspection

At Arrow, we understand that the home inspection is just one part of a much larger journey—and our role is to provide clear, accurate information that helps buyers and sellers make informed decisions.

We're not here to sway a deal one way or another. Our job is to offer a detailed snapshot of the home's current condition so that you, as the agent, can guide your client confidently through whatever next step they choose.

We recognize that strong, well-written offers should stand on their own, and inspections aren't meant to be used as leverage from the outset. Instead, the inspection helps your client—whether buyer or seller—understand what's in front of them, so they can decide what feels right based on their goals and comfort level.

We've seen that when agents and inspectors work together with mutual respect and clarity of roles, clients feel empowered, not overwhelmed. Our aim is to be a trusted resource in that process, providing the insights, so you can provide the strategy.

We know inspections can sometimes feel like they put everyone on edge, but that's never our intent. Inspections aren't designed to "find everything wrong," they're meant to provide a snapshot in time that helps clients make informed choices. When that information is framed with the right context, it shifts the conversation from fear to forward momentum. It's not about perfection; it's about progress. And when a client walks away feeling empowered and confident in their decision, that's a reflection of the strong partnership between a thoughtful agent and a clear inspection. That's exactly the kind of outcome we're here to support.

Let's Get Straight to the Point...

This book was written to help buyers, sellers, and agents better understand the home inspection process; not just what, but the why. Each chapter will break down a different part of the home, from foundations to roofs, plumbing to electrical, helping you know what to expect, what matters most, and what to do next. You'll learn how to interpret inspection findings, ask the right questions, and plan for repairs or upgrades without panic. Whether you're new to real estate or have bought and sold before, this book is here to give you confidence, clarity, and a realistic understanding of how to keep a home safe, functional, and standing strong for the next generation.

Chapter One

Roofing

What's Over Your Head and Why You Should Pay Attention

THE ROOF IS ONE of the most critical systems in your home. During a home inspection, the roof is evaluated for condition, safety, and function, including its covering (like shingles or tiles), drainage (gutters and downspouts), flashing (the protective metal pieces around seams and edges), vents, chimneys, and any other penetrations or protrusions.

While inspectors often walk the roof if it's safe to do so, they may also assess it from the ground, ladders, or accessible eaves. The goal is to identify visible wear, potential leaks, safety hazards, or signs of improper installation without causing damage or removing materials.

The slope (or pitch) of a roof also plays a major role in how well it sheds water and what type of roofing materials are appropriate. In case your inspector uses industry jargon, here's a quick breakdown: roof pitch is expressed as a ratio like 4/12 or 6/12, meaning the roof rises 4 or 6 inches for every 12 inches it runs across. Think of it like the slope of a triangle.

- Low-slope roofs (2/12 and below) need materials that can handle standing water, like rubber or rolled roofing.
- Moderate to steep-slope roofs (3/12 and up) are well-suited for shingles, tiles, and metal roofing, which rely on gravity to direct water away.

Using the right material for the pitch is essential otherwise, you risk premature wear, leaks, or pooling. Your inspector can tell you the pitch of your roof and whether the current materials are a good fit.

Common roof types inspected include:

- Asphalt Shingles: The most common; available in 3-tab (budget-friendly, thinner) or architectural (thicker, more durable and dimensional).
- Metal Roofing: Long-lasting and energy-efficient, but can have flashing and seam issues.
- Rubber/EPDM Roofing: Common on low-slope or flat roofs; prone to seam separation and ponding.
- Wood Shingles or Shakes: Attractive, but require frequent maintenance and are vulnerable to moisture.
- Clay/Slate Tiles: High-end, heavy, and long-lasting—but costly to repair and inspect.

Why the Roof Matters

The roof does more than keep you dry, it protects the entire structure of your home. A compromised roof can lead to:

- Water intrusion and interior damage
- Mold and decay in attics and walls
- Compromised insulation and rising energy costs
- Foundation issues caused by improper water drainage
- Possible insurance denials or lender refusals to finance a property

Early detection of roofing issues helps avoid costly repairs and ensures a safer, healthier home.

What Clients Should Understand

Here are the most common concerns found during roof inspections and what they mean:

- Aging shingles: Shingles may curl, crack, or shed granules (the bumpy parts of the shingles) as they age. Ask how many years are left based on the roof's material and condition.
- Ridge caps and soft spots: Signs of structural wear. Ridge caps help shed water at the roof's peak, while soft spots may indicate hidden damage.
- Moss and algae: These may look harmless but retain mois-

ture and accelerate deterioration. Regular cleaning or professional soft washing is recommended.

- Loose or damaged flashing: Flashing around chimneys, skylights, or plumbing and stack vents should be properly sealed. Improper flashing is one of the leading causes of roof leaks.
- Short or blocked chimneys/vents: Often impacted by the design of your roof, these can cause exhaust gases to re-enter the home. Adequate height and airflow are essential.
- Gutters and downspouts: Working with the design and pitch of your roof, debris buildup prevents water from draining, leading to possible roof and subsequent foundation problems.
- Overhanging trees: Branches can rub against shingles or trap moisture (often as simple as preventing sunlight from burning off water from rain) leading to wear and water penetration.

What to Ask Your Inspector

When your roof is being inspected, consider asking:

- What is the estimated remaining life of the roof?
- Are there signs of improper installation or past repairs?
- Do any areas need immediate attention or can they be monitored over time?

- Is the attic properly ventilated to prevent heat/moisture buildup?
- Are flashing and chimney penetrations sealed and functional?
- Are gutters and downspouts directing water away from the home effectively?
- Is there anything about the roof style or slope that presents future concerns?

How Arrow Home Inspections Supports You

When you book with Arrow Home Inspections, your standard home inspection includes a comprehensive visual evaluation of the roof system. This covers:

- Roofing materials, visible wear, and drainage and Arrow Home Inspections ALWAYS go on the roof to make these observations. It is not common for inspectors to go on the roof and not all things can be seen from the ground.
- Flashing, penetrations, and chimney integrity
- Ventilation systems and plumbing stack vents
- Gutter performance and debris assessment
- Photos and clear, same-day reporting on roof condition

If issues are identified, Arrow can provide:

- A recommendation to contact a roofing professional for further evaluation or repair
- Guidance on the next steps for cleaning, repairs, or replacements
- Digital access to videos or articles via QR code to help you understand common findings
- Peace of mind: if something looks unfamiliar or intimidating, we'll break it down in plain English

Frequent Flyers on the Inspection Report

Roof issues are some of the most common findings in home inspections. While they can seem intimidating at first glance, nearly all of them are fixable. Roofs naturally age and wear over time, and small concerns can be excellent indicators that regular maintenance or repair is due. It's not unusual to uncover these issues—and catching them early is key.

Common Findings:

- Missing or Damaged Shingles: Can lead to leaks but are usually localized and easily replaced.
- Improper Flashing: Often found around chimneys, skylights, or roof edges; replacing or sealing flashing is a routine repair.

- Granule Loss on Asphalt Shingles: Normal as shingles age; may signal it's time to monitor the roof's condition more closely.
- Moss or Algae Growth: Common in shaded areas; can be cleaned and prevented with proper ventilation and roof care.
- Signs of Past Leaks: Water stains or patching inside the attic or on ceilings are often resolved once the source is identified.

Final Thought: Be Proactive, Not Reactive

Your roof isn't just shingles, it's a shield. Knowing its age, condition, and weak points helps you make informed decisions before you buy and prepare for future upkeep. Whether you're concerned about a short vent, moss buildup, or simply want to know how long your current roof will last, a thorough inspection with Arrow Home Inspections gets you straight to the point.

Roofing Terms Made Simple

Asphalt Shingles: The most common roofing material. Available in 3-tab (flat, thinner).

Architectural Shingles: A premium type of asphalt shingle with a layered look and longer lifespan than 3-tab shingles.

3-Tab Shingles: A basic, budget-friendly asphalt shingle with a flat, uniform appearance.

Roof Pitch: : The steepness of a roof, shown as a ratio (e.g., 4/12 means it rises 4 inches for every 12 inches across).

Low-Slope Roof: A gently sloped roof (2/12 and below) that requires special waterproof materials.

Ridge: The top edge or peak where two roof slopes meet. Covered by ridge cap shingles.

Gable: The triangular section of wall under the ends of a sloped roof. Often seen on the sides of houses.

Eave: The lower edge of the roof that overhangs the exterior wall—where gutters are attached.

Soffit: The underside of the eave, visible when you look up from under the roof edge. Helps ventilate the attic.

Fascia: The flat board (trim piece) that is runs along the roof edge, directly behind the gutters. NOTE: Does not provide structural support.

Valley: The "V"-shaped trough where two sloped roof sections meet. Directs water runoff and is prone to leaks.

Hip: The external angle formed where two sloping roof sections meet, often seen on all sides of a hip-style roof.

Flashing: Thin metal installed around roof openings (like chimneys and vents) or seams to prevent water leaks.

Roof Deck (Sheathing): The base layer of the roof, usually plywood or OSB where roofing materials are applied.

Underlayment: A protective barrier between the roof deck and shingles that helps prevent moisture penetration.

Gutters: Channels along the eaves that collect and direct rainwater away from the house.

Downspouts: Pipes that carry water from the gutters down to the ground and away from the foundation.

Moss: A moisture-retaining plant that can grow on shingles and lead to faster roof deterioration.

Soft Spot: A spongy or weakened area on the roof surface that may indicate rot or water damage.

EPDM/TPO Roofing: EPDM (Ethylene Propylene Diene Monomer) and TPO (Thermoplastic Polyolefin) Rubber or synthetic roofing materials used on flat or low-slope roofs for waterproofing.

Explore Real-World Inspection Insights

Want to see what our inspectors actually find in the field? Visit our page for real photos and helpful context, organized by the same sections you've just read about. Whether you're buying, selling, or just curious, this gallery gives you a behind-the-scenes look at what we see or how to spot issues before they become problems.

Start exploring at *Inspection Insights:* ***arrow-homeinspections.com/inspection-insights*** or scan the QR code at the end of each chapter.

Roof and Chimney

Chapter Two

What to Know About Chimneys

More Than Just a Stack of Bricks

Chimneys may look simple from the outside, but they play a critical role in both ventilation and safety. Depending on your home, a chimney may vent your fireplace, your heating system (like a furnace or boiler), or your water heater and sometimes more than one at the same time. That's why chimney issues can affect everything from indoor air quality and energy efficiency to fire risk and structural integrity.

What to Look for in a Chimney

Whether your chimney is brick, block, or metal, there are a few essential components and warning signs every client should understand:

Materials Matter

- Masonry chimneys (brick or stone) are durable but can suffer from cracked mortar joints, flaking, or spalling bricks (a condition where the surface of the brick chips, flakes, or breaks off due to moisture damage and freeze-thaw cycles).

- Metal chimneys and lined flues can corrode or come apart at the seams, especially if not sealed properly or exposed to long-term moisture.
- Chimney crowns (also called cement caps) are the concrete tops that seal off the top of a masonry chimney structure. If they crack or deteriorate, water can enter the chimney and cause damage to the flue or even leak into the home.
- Chimney caps are the metal covers above the crown that keep rain, snow, animals, and debris out of the flue itself. Without one, your chimney is an open invitation to water intrusion, nests, and blockages.

Flashing

- Flashing is the metal barrier that seals the gap between the chimney and the roof. Damaged or poorly installed flashing is one of the top causes of roof leaks.
- Look for rust, lifting edges, or visible gaps around the base of the chimney.

Height and Draft

- Chimney height matters especially in how it affects airflow, or draft (the natural upward flow of air, smoke, and gases through the chimney flue. It's created when warm air from a fireplace, furnace, or water heater rises and pulls cooler air behind it). A chimney that's too short may struggle to vent properly, especially when placed in the center of the roof where air turbulence is strongest.

- Improper drafting can allow dangerous gases like carbon monoxide to linger in the home instead of being safely vented outside.

Shared Venting

- Some chimneys vent more than one appliance (like a fireplace and furnace). This isn't always a problem, but it must be properly designed.
- If the flue is too small, too large, or shared improperly, it can cause back-drafting (as you can imagine, this is when exhaust gases like smoke or carbon monoxide flow back into the home instead of safely going up and out through the chimney or vent) or allow heat damage to the liner or walls.

The 2-10 Rule: Proper Chimney Height

- Chimneys must extend at least 2 feet higher than anything within 10 feet horizontally.
- The top of the chimney must be at least 3 feet above the roof where it exits.
- Proper height helps prevent downdrafts and ensures safe, effective ventilation.
- Chimneys that don't meet this standard may need to be extended or upgraded.

What Clients Should Understand

Chimneys are not just decorative, they're part of your home's mechanical and safety systems.

Chimney issues are often hidden. Many problems happen inside the flue, not where you can easily see them.

If your heating system or water heater vents into a chimney, it's crucial to confirm the flue is sized, lined, and functioning properly.

Side-mounted chimneys (on the exterior wall) sometimes draft more reliably than center-of-roof chimneys, but placement isn't the only factor that matters.

A missing chimney cap allows rain, snow, and animals to enter leading to moisture damage, corrosion, and blockages.

A cracked chimney crown is often the first failure point in a masonry chimney and can lead to widespread water damage if ignored.

Spalling bricks are an early indicator of water damage, catching them early can save thousands in structural repairs.

The "Other" Types of Chimneys: Direct Vent & PVC Exhaust Systems

Not all chimneys are built from brick or stone. Many newer homes, or homes with upgraded heating systems, may not have a traditional chimney at all. Instead, they use direct vent or PVC exhaust systems to safely remove combustion gases from high-efficiency appliances like furnaces, boilers, or on-demand water heaters.

These systems:

- Are made of white or gray PVC piping and typically vent horizontally through an exterior wall, rather than through the roof.
- Often include both intake and exhaust pipes, ensuring a sealed and balanced system that doesn't draw air from inside the home.
- Do not rely on chimney drafts and are often mechanically assisted with fans or blowers.
- Must be sloped correctly (usually slightly downward toward the unit to prevent outside water intrusion) and terminate safely away from doors, windows, or vents.
- Require secure fittings and clearances, especially in cold climates where condensation can freeze and block airflow.

If your home uses this type of system, Arrow Home Inspections will:

- Verify the visible PVC piping is intact and properly supported
- Confirm exhaust vents aren't too close to walkways, windows, or fresh air intakes
- Suggest professional evaluation if vent pipes appear loose, obstructed, or incorrectly sloped

These systems may look simpler than a brick chimney but they require proper installation and maintenance to perform safely and efficiently.

What to Ask Your Inspector

- Is the chimney structurally sound and free of visible cracks or leaning?
- Is the flashing properly sealed to prevent roof leaks?
- Is there a chimney cap and crown, and are they in good condition?
- Is the chimney tall enough for proper drafting based on its location and use?
- Does the chimney vent multiple systems, and are they vented correctly?
- Would you recommend a chimney sweep or specialist to evaluate the internal flue condition?

How Arrow Home Inspections Supports You

Arrow Home Inspections includes a visual chimney assessment as part of every full home inspection.

Our inspection includes:

- Identifying visible cracks, wear, or leaning
- Checking for proper flashing and crown condition
- Verifying that a chimney cap is present and functional
- Evaluating chimney height, slope, and structural integrity

- Noting signs of blockage, deterioration, or shared venting concerns

If further evaluation is needed, we will suggest you hire a trusted professional for:

- Flue camera inspections
- Draft testing and airflow analysis
- Cap and crown installation or replacement
- Masonry repair or full chimney restoration

Frequent Flyers on the Inspection Report

Chimneys are often overlooked until problems arise, but they play a crucial role in home ventilation and safety. Fortunately, most chimney issues are relatively simple to repair or manage once identified. Inspections can reveal conditions that have slowly developed over time, many of which are common and correctable.

Common Findings:

- Missing or Damaged Chimney Cap: A quick and inexpensive fix that prevents water and animals from entering.
- Cracked or Spalling Bricks: Often due to water exposure; repairs may involve repointing or replacing bricks.
- Deteriorated Crown: The cement cap on top can crack with age but is usually easy to resurface or rebuild.

- Improper Drafting: May require chimney height adjustments or a new cap; solvable with guidance from a qualified professional.
- Damaged or Rusted Flashing: Causes leaks at the roof line; repairable without replacing the chimney.

Final Thought: Respect the Stack

Chimneys might be out of sight, but they should never be out of mind. Whether they're venting cozy fires or critical systems like your water heater or furnace, a compromised chimney can cause moisture problems, poor indoor air quality, and even health hazards. Arrow Home Inspections helps ensure your chimney is safe, sound, and doing its job so you can enjoy your home with peace of mind.

Chimney Terms Made Simple

Chimney Cap: A metal covering placed at the top of a chimney to prevent water, animals, and debris from entering the flue.

Cement Cap: A concrete layer that sits on top of a masonry chimney to seal the structure and shed water.

Flue: The interior passage inside the chimney that carries smoke or exhaust gases safely out of the home.

Flue Liner: A protective lining inside the flue (usually clay, metal, or ceramic) that insulates and protects the chimney structure. Of Special

Note: Homes built prior to the 1950's typically do not have a liner. Ask your inspector about your specific home and the need for a liner.

Spalling Bricks: Bricks that are flaking, cracking, or chipping due to moisture damage, often caused by freeze-thaw cycles.

Flashing (Chimney): Metal sealing between the chimney base and the roof to prevent leaks.

Draft: The upward flow of air and gases through the chimney. Poor draft means gases may not exit properly.

Back-Drafting: When exhaust gases flow back into the home instead of being vented outside—often a safety concern.

Shared Venting: When more than one appliance (like a furnace and fireplace) vents through the same chimney. Must be properly designed.

Masonry Chimney: A chimney built of brick or stone—durable but susceptible to moisture damage if not maintained.

Metal Chimney: A factory-built metal venting system used for certain fireplaces or heating systems. Often seen on newer or modular homes.

Explore Real-World Inspection Insights

Want to see what our inspectors actually find in the field? Visit our page for real photos and helpful context, organized by the same sections you've just read about. Whether you're buying, selling, or just curious, this gallery gives you a behind-the-scenes look at what we see or how to spot issues before they become problems.

Start exploring at Inspection Insights: arrow-homeinspections.com/inspection-insights or scan the QR code at the end of each chapter.

Roof and Chimney

Chapter Three

Exterior Elements

First Impressions, Lasting Protection

The exterior of a home does more than define its curb appeal, it serves as the first line of defense against the elements. From siding and trim to stairs, decks, doors, and railings, these components work together to protect your home's structure, preserve energy efficiency, and ensure safety for everyone entering and exiting the property.

During the exterior inspection, Arrow Home Inspections looks at a wide range of visible elements, including:

- Siding, trim, soffits, and fascia
- Exterior doors and windows
- Decks, stoops, stairs, and porches
- Railings and balusters
- Gutters and downspouts (yes, again)
- Exterior electrical outlets, dryer vents, and faucets

The goal is to assess these components for signs of wear, safety concerns, or structural issues helping clients understand what may need repair, what's functioning as intended, and what could impact the integrity or livability of the home.

Why Exterior Elements Matter

These elements work together to:

- Keep water and pests out of the home
- Maintain proper drainage and ventilation
- Provide safe entry and exit for residents and guests
- Support the overall structure and appearance of the home
- Prevent long-term damage caused by moisture, neglect, or aging materials

Neglecting exterior maintenance can lead to hidden water damage, pest intrusion, energy inefficiency, and costly repairs down the line.

What Clients Should Understand

Here are the most common exterior concerns and what they mean:

Siding & Trim

- Common siding materials in New England include wood shingles, vinyl, fiber cement (like Hardie board), and brick veneer. Each has different maintenance needs and lifespan expectations.

- Wood shingles offer classic charm but require regular painting or staining and are prone to rot or insect damage.
- Vinyl siding is low-maintenance and resistant to moisture, but it can crack in cold weather and may fade over time.
- Aluminum siding is metal siding material popular from the 1940s to 1970s. Lightweight and rust-resistant, but prone to denting and paint chalking over time. Still found on many older homes in urban areas like Boston.
- Fiber cement is durable, fire-resistant, and holds paint well, but it's heavier and may need occasional repainting.
- Brick veneer requires minimal maintenance but can develop mortar cracks or efflorescence (white powdery buildup).
- Look for signs of cracking, rot, peeling paint, or warping.
- Damaged siding can lead to water infiltration and mold.

Doors & Windows

- Poorly sealed doors or windows can cause drafts, moisture intrusion, and higher energy bills.
- Broken or boarded-up windows should be replaced—not only for functionality, but also for safety and security.
- Storm doors that don't close properly may not protect against weather or energy loss.

Window Trim and Flashing

- Missing or deteriorated flashing can lead to leaks around windows and door frames.
- Flashing and caulking should be intact to keep moisture out.

Stairs, Stoops & Railings

- Cracked or spalling concrete (when the surface chips or flakes) can be a tripping hazard or sign of moisture damage.
- Railings with baluster spacing over 4 inches can pose a fall risk, especially for children.
- Stairs with uneven riser heights can be unsafe and a tripping or fall hazard.
- Stairs should have proper footings at the base to ensure long-term support and prevent shifting or settling.
- Staircases should also include a center stringer to provide additional support and prevent sagging or movement.

Decks & Porches

- Decks must be evaluated for structural stability especially if the underside isn't visible.
- Wood rot, warped treads, or loose railings can make a deck unsafe for regular use.
- Inspect how the deck is attached to the house ideally using a ledger board secured with lag bolts, not just nails.

- Decks must be properly flashed to prevent water from seeping between the house and the deck's ledger board. Without proper flashing, moisture can infiltrate the wall, leading to rot, mold, and structural damage to both the deck and the home.

- Check that the deck is supported by proper footings, such as concrete piers (vertical supports made of poured concrete used to support the weight of a deck, porch, or other structure. They serve as footings that transfer the structure's load into the ground) or blocks, rather than resting directly on soil or unanchored materials.

- In colder states (like New England) concrete piers must be installed below the local frost line typically 42" deep, depending on the region. This is typically done to prevent frost heaving, which can lift, shift, or crack structures over time due to the expansion and contraction of frozen ground.

Downspouts & Roof Drains

- Downspouts are the vertical pipes that connect to the gutters and carry water down to ground level.

- Roof drains are typically found on flat or low-slope roofs and connect to interior piping or scuppers to manage water runoff.

- Extensions or diverters should be used to prevent water from pooling near the foundation.

- These should direct water away from the home's foundation. Water should be discharged at least 4–6 feet away from the home or directed into a drainage system

- Clogged or misdirected downspouts can lead to basement leaks or soil erosion.

Exterior Electrical Outlets & Faucets

- GFCI (Ground Fault Circuit Interrupter) outlets are required outdoors for safety.
- Faucets should be functional and not leaking (winterized systems may not be testable in cold months).
- Dryer vents should be clear and cleaned regularly to prevent fire hazards.

What to Ask Your Inspector

- Is the siding or trim damaged or showing signs of rot?
- How much "life" is left in the trim? How much "life" is left in the trim pieces?
- Are there any issues with railings, steps, or walkways that could affect safety of use?
- Are windows and doors properly sealed and secure?
- Does the deck or porch show signs of wear, warping, or water damage?
- Are downspouts draining properly away from the home's foundation?

- Are GFCI outlets and exterior lighting functioning as they should?
- Is any exterior flashing or caulking missing or damaged?

How Arrow Home Inspections Supports You

Arrow Home Inspections thoroughly evaluates visible and accessible exterior elements as part of every home inspection. This includes:

- A full visual assessment of siding, trim, windows, doors, stairs, and decks
- Documentation of safety issues (like loose railings or trip hazards)
- Noting materials used and signs of rot, warping, or improper construction
- Observing how exterior elements may be impacting water management or structural integrity

Need more certainty? We'll recommend qualified professionals for:

- Siding replacement or repair
- Window and door installation
- Masonry or concrete restoration
- Deck rebuilding or reinforcement
- Electrical and plumbing support for outdoor systems

Frequent Flyers on the Inspection Report

Your home's exterior is its first line of defense against the elements—and it naturally takes the most wear. From siding to stairs, inspectors frequently find signs of weather exposure, age, or improper installation. The good news? These issues are usually cosmetic or maintenance-related and can be resolved with standard repair work or upkeep.

Common Findings:

• Damaged or Rotting Siding/Trim – Wood and composite siding may show signs of decay or peeling. Often resolved with patching, repainting, or replacing small sections.

• Loose or Worn Railings – Railings may become wobbly or have wide baluster gaps. This is a common safety concern but easily fixed by reinforcing or upgrading.

• Boarded or Damaged Windows – Especially in older homes, cracked panes or missing sashes are typical and can be replaced or repaired.

• Spalling Concrete Steps – Freeze-thaw cycles often cause concrete chipping. Patching or resurfacing can restore safety and appearance.

• Inadequate Deck Flashing or Attachment – Improperly connected decks can lead to moisture intrusion. Repairs may involve adding lag bolts or flashing to secure and protect the ledger board.

Final Thought: Small Fixes, Big Peace of Mind

A cracked stair or warped door frame might not seem like a big deal but small issues on the outside can hint at bigger problems underneath. Arrow Home Inspections helps you spot these concerns early, so you can move forward with confidence, plan for repairs if needed, and make informed decisions about your home's maintenance.

Exterior Elements Made Simple

Siding: The outer wall covering of a home (e.g., wood shingles, vinyl, fiber cement) that protects against weather and provides insulation.

Trim: The finishing materials around windows, doors, and corners of a house—often decorative but also protective.

Fascia: The horizontal board along the edge of the roof where gutters are attached.

Soffit: The underside of the roof overhang (eave); it allows airflow into the attic for ventilation.

Flashing: Thin metal installed above windows, doors, and joints to prevent water from seeping in.

Stoop: A small entry platform or step at a doorway, often made of concrete or masonry.

Baluster: The vertical posts between stair or porch railings. Spacing wider than 4 inches can be a safety concern.

Railing: A barrier or guard along stairs, decks, or porches to prevent falls. Required by code for certain heights. Installed at 36" on the first floor and 42" second floors and above.

Spalling: When concrete or brick chips, flakes, or crumbles usually from moisture damage or freeze-thaw cycles.

GFCI Outlet: A Ground Fault Circuit Interrupter outlet that protects against electrical shock. Required for outdoor use.

Storm Door: A secondary door installed outside an exterior door to improve insulation and protect against weather.

Dryer Vent: An exterior opening that releases hot air and moisture from a clothes dryer. It must be kept clear to prevent fire risk.

Deck Stringers: The angled structural supports under a deck staircase that hold up the steps.

Riser Height: The vertical space between one stair tread and the next. Inconsistent heights can be a trip hazard.

Downspout: A pipe that carries rainwater from the roof gutters down to the ground and away from the house.

Ledger Board: The structural component that connects a deck to the house.

Footings: Concrete bases located beneath structural supports like decks or stairs. In colder climates, they must be installed below the frost line to prevent frost heave, which can cause shifting or cracking over time. Footings help distribute the weight of a structure safely into the ground.

Center Stringer: A middle support board beneath a staircase, running from the top step to the base. It provides additional strength and prevents sagging, especially on wider staircases where two side stringers alone may not offer enough support.

Explore Real-World Inspection Insights

Want to see what our inspectors actually find in the field? Visit our page for real photos and helpful context, organized by the same sections you've just read about. Whether you're buying, selling, or just curious, this gallery gives you a behind-the-scenes look at what we see or how to spot issues before they become problems.

Start exploring at Inspection Insights: arrow-homeinspections.com/inspection-insights or scan the QR code at the end of each chapter.

Exterior and Site Elements

Chapter Four

Site Elements

What's Beneath Your Feet Can Impact What's Above

WHEN YOU THINK OF a home inspection, your mind may go straight to the roof, the foundation, or the plumbing but the land around the house matters just as much. The condition of driveways, walkways, grading, and vegetation all play a major role in the long-term health of the home.

Even small issues on the outside, like uneven ground or tree roots, can lead to water damage, structural stress, or trip hazards. That's why evaluating the site is a key part of every home inspection.

A Brief Overview

During the inspection of site elements, Arrow Home Inspections assesses the exterior areas around the home that could affect its structure, safety, or drainage. This includes:

- Grading and surface drainage

- Driveways and walkways
- Retaining walls and slopes
- Landscaping and overgrown vegetation
- Trip hazards, soil erosion, and settlement cracks

The inspector looks for how water flows around the property, whether the landscaping is too close to the structure, and if hard surfaces are stable and in good condition.

Why Site Elements Matter

Problems with site elements may seem cosmetic, but they often lead to:

- Water intrusion in basements or crawlspaces
- Soil erosion that undermines the foundation or walkways
- Cracked driveways that become safety issues
- Tree roots or overgrowth that damage siding, roofs, or underground utilities
- Poor grading that directs water toward the house instead of away

Keeping the site in good condition helps preserve the home and makes it safer and more enjoyable to live in.

What Clients Should Understand

Here are some of the most common site concerns and what they mean:

Grading and Drainage (* See Special Section Spotlight)

- The ground should slope away from the house to keep water from pooling near the foundation.
- Flat or negative grading can lead to water seepage into basements or crawlspaces.
- Look for standing water, erosion channels, or mulch that has washed away after rain.

Driveways and Walkways

- Cracks, heaving, or uneven pavers can be trip hazards or signs of settling soil.
- Pay attention to areas where water collects—especially if they slope toward the house.
- Asphalt, concrete, and stone surfaces all have different maintenance needs and lifespans.

Vegetation and Landscaping

- Trees and bushes planted too close to the home can cause damage to siding, roofs, or foundations. All vegetation should be cut back to 16" from the house to prevent insect and moisture intrusion.
- Roots can grow into foundations or sewer lines, and over-

hanging branches can damage shingles or gutters.

- Plants should be trimmed back and not touch the structure.

Retaining Walls

- These help manage sloped land and prevent soil movement.
- Inspectors look for bulging, cracking, or leaning, which can be signs of failure or poor drainage behind the wall.
- Proper drainage (weep holes or gravel backfill) is key to preventing wall collapse.

***Spotlight: Negative Grading: Common, Costly, and Easy to Fix**

Negative grading, when the ground slopes *toward* the home instead of *away*, is one of the most common issues inspectors find during a site evaluation. The good news? It's also one of the simplest problems to correct with basic landscaping work.

Why It's a Problem:

- Directs rainwater and snowmelt toward the foundation, increasing the risk of:
    - Basement leaks
    - Foundation cracks
    - Mold and mildew in crawlspaces or lower levels
- Promotes soil erosion and pooling near the home's perimeter

- Can lead to pest intrusion, especially in damp or soft ground near siding

Simple Fixes for Homeowners:

- Add soil or top dressing to create a gentle slope (at least 6 inches of drop over 10 feet away from the home)
- Use landscaping fabric and mulch to help with drainage and control erosion
- Extend downspouts to discharge water at least 4–6 feet from the foundation
- Install a French drain or swale (a low-lying, usually wet, area of land, often a shallow depression or a channel for directing water runoff. Swales are frequently found along roadsides, in fields, or as part of drainage systems).
- Avoid piling mulch or flower beds too high against the house, which can trap moisture

Tip: Walk around your home after a rainstorm. If you see water pooling next to the foundation, it's time to check your grading. Correcting negative grading early helps prevent much bigger and more expensive repairs down the line.

What to Ask Your Inspector

- Is the grading sufficient to move water away from the foundation?

- Are there visible signs of erosion or water pooling on the property?
- Are the walkways or driveway in good condition and sloped correctly?
- Are trees or vegetation too close to the house or roofline?
- Are retaining walls structurally sound and draining properly?

How Arrow Home Inspections Supports You

Arrow Home Inspections evaluates the condition of all visible and accessible site elements. We look for:

- Drainage concerns or poor grading
- Trip hazards and uneven walking surfaces
- Cracking or settlement in hardscapes
- Vegetation-related risks
- Structural issues with retaining walls

We'll document our findings clearly in your report and let you know if further evaluation or correction is needed. When problems are found, we'll recommend:

- Drainage solutions (grading, French drains, extensions)

- Tree or root management by a licensed arborist
- Surface repair by a qualified mason or paving company
- Retaining wall reinforcement or rebuilding by structural professionals

Frequent Flyers on the Inspection Report

Site grading and drainage often fly under the radar, but they play a vital role in protecting your home from moisture damage and foundation issues. The good news? These problems are not only common—they're also typically easy to fix. Most homeowners can prevent major issues with a bit of maintenance and some dirt in the right place. Remember: common issues are just that—common—and rarely cause for panic when addressed early.

Common Findings:

• Negative Grading – Soil slopes toward the foundation instead of away from it. Often corrected by adding or reshaping soil.

• Clogged or Short Downspouts – Water discharges too close to the house. Easily fixed with extensions or splash blocks.

• Improper Swales – Poorly formed drainage channels that cause pooling or runoff issues. May need reshaping to redirect water.

• Settling Around the Foundation – Creates low spots that collect water. Can usually be corrected with fill soil and compaction.

• Overgrown Vegetation Near Foundation – Blocks airflow and holds moisture. Trimming or relocating plants can improve drainage and reduce moisture risks.

Final Thought: Keep the Ground in Check

Your home isn't just four walls, it's part of the land it sits on. When that land doesn't drain well, isn't maintained, or shifts over time, it can create real problems. A solid inspection of your site elements gives you peace of mind and helps you prioritize any landscaping or hardscaping projects wisely.

Site Elements Made Simple

Grading: The slope of the ground around a home. Proper grading slopes away from the structure to prevent water pooling.

Drainage: The way water flows and moves away from the property, especially during rain. Poor drainage can lead to basement leaks or erosion.

Retaining Wall: A structure (often made of concrete, stone, or timber) used to hold back soil on sloped lots.

Weep Hole: A small opening in a retaining wall that allows water to drain out, preventing pressure buildup behind the wall.

Surface Erosion: The wearing away of topsoil or landscaping due to water runoff. Often leaves exposed roots or washout paths.

Settlement Cracks: Cracks in pavement, concrete, or walls caused by soil shifting beneath them. Common near foundations or walkways.

Negative Grading When the land slopes toward the home, increasing the risk of water intrusion into the foundation.

Hardscape: The non-living parts of landscaping—like patios, driveways, walkways, and retaining walls.

Root Intrusion: When tree roots grow into structures or systems like foundations, pipes, or walkways, causing damage.

Swale: A low-lying, usually wet, area of land, often a shallow depression or a channel for directing water runoff. Swales are frequently found along roadsides, in fields, or as part of drainage systems.

Explore Real-World Inspection Insights

Want to see what our inspectors actually find in the field? Visit our page for real photos and helpful context, organized by the same sections you've just read about. Whether you're buying, selling, or just curious, this gallery gives you a behind-the-scenes look at what we see or how to spot issues before they become problems.

Start exploring at Inspection Insights: arrow-homeinspections.com/inspection-insights or scan the QR code at the end of each chapter.

Exterior and Site Elements

Chapter Five

Structural Elements

The Frame That Holds It All Together

THE STRENGTH AND SAFETY of any home depend on its structure. While walls, siding, and flooring are what you see every day, it's the underlying beams, columns, and foundation that provide lasting support. A structural issue whether due to age, poor construction, or environmental conditions can be costly to repair and even dangerous if left unaddressed.

That's why the structural elements of a home are one of the most important parts of any inspection.

A Brief Overview

During a structural evaluation, Arrow Home Inspections focuses on the visible, load-bearing components of the home, including:

- Foundation walls (concrete, stone, block, brick, granite)
- Floor joists, beams, and support columns

- Visible framing in basements or crawlspaces
- Structural movement (settling, cracking, bowing)
- Support piers or posts
- Attic and roof framing

The goal is to assess whether the home's framework is stable, properly supported, and free from active movement or deterioration. Inspections are visual and non-invasive, but they can identify early warning signs of structural problems.

Why Structural Elements Matter

If the structural components of a home are compromised, you could face:

- Uneven floors, sagging ceilings, or cracked walls
- Water intrusion and wood decay, especially in basements or crawlspaces
- Foundation settlement or movement
- Major repair costs if framing or supports need replacement
- Safety risks from improperly supported floors or walls

These issues may reduce a home's value, interfere with renovations, and could affect insurance or loan approval.

What Clients Should Understand

Foundations

- Most homes in the Northeast have concrete, fieldstone, brick, slab (* see special section), or block foundations. Here is what to keep an eye out for:
    - Concrete Foundation Cracks: Hairline cracks are common and often due to settling, but wider or stair-step cracks may indicate settling, shifting, or water pressure. Arrow inspectors look for active movement and signs of seepage.
    - Fieldstone Foundation Imperfections: Look for gaps between stones, signs of bulging or bowing, crumbling mortar, and water infiltration. These are common in older homes and may indicate settlement, moisture issues, or the need for repointing to maintain stability.
    - Slab Foundation Concerns: Since there's no crawlspace or basement, shifting or cracks in a slab may directly affect interior flooring. Look for uneven floors, separation at baseboards, or visible slab cracks, which may hint at moisture or structural issues below.
    - Block Foundation Issues: Common in mid-century homes, block foundations may show horizontal cracking or bowing from exterior pressure. Mortar joint deterioration, movement, or water staining between blocks can point to structural compromise.
- In any foundation, look for horizontal or step cracks or signs

of moisture as these may indicate movement or seepage.

- Small vertical cracks are common in older homes and often not structural, but they should be monitored.

Beams, Columns, and Joists

- Support beams carry the load of the house across wide spans.
- Joists are the horizontal boards that hold up floors or ceilings.
- Posts or columns supporting beams, should rest on solid footings, not directly on soil or slab.
- Wood beams or supports should be free from decay, insect damage, or sagging.
- Columns supporting structural elements such as carrying beams should be lally columns, not temporary supports like screw jacks, unless the product is specifically rated for permanent use.

Framing in Basements and Crawlspaces

- Exposed framing should be dry and solid.
- Signs of moisture, staining, or decay can weaken structural integrity.
- In crawlspaces, moisture and poor ventilation can lead to mold, wood decay, and foundation issues.

Signs of Settlement or Movement

- Diagonal cracks above windows or doors

- Doors or windows that stick or don't close evenly
- Sloped or bouncy floors
- Gaps between walls and baseboards

Not all cracks mean trouble but your inspector will determine if they're cosmetic or structural in nature.

Spotlight on Structure: Slab Ranches and Truss-Based Framing*

Not all slab ranch homes are built the same. While all share a concrete slab foundation with no basement or crawl space, their framing systems can differ significantly especially when it comes to how the roof load is supported.

One common variation features a truss-based roof system, which transfers the structural load entirely to the exterior walls. These homes typically do not have interior load-bearing walls, allowing for:

- Easier wall removal or open-concept layouts
- Simpler remodeling and layout changes
- Faster and more efficient original construction

However, any modification to the trusses such as cutting, notching, or altering to vault ceilings can compromise structural integrity. Arrow inspectors always check for visible signs of damage, sagging, or unauthorized alterations.

Key Considerations for Slab Ranches:

- Foundation: Built directly on a concrete slab with no basement. Original radiant heating may be embedded in the slab; some systems still function, while others were replaced with forced air or baseboard heat.

- Mechanical Access: Plumbing and HVAC lines often run through the attic or perimeter walls, making upgrades and repairs more challenging.

- Comfort: Slabs may have minimal insulation beneath, leading to colder floors and limited options for insulation improvement.

- Additions: Rear additions or enclosed garages are common in slab ranches. Arrow checks for issues like structural separation, slab cracking, and insulation mismatches.

Whether slab ranches use a truss system or traditional framing with load-bearing interior walls, Arrow Home Inspections evaluates each structure's integrity and suitability for renovation. Our goal is to help you understand how the home was built and how it can perform in the future.

What to Ask Your Inspector

- Are there any visible signs of foundation movement or damage?

- Are the support posts and beams adequately sized and properly installed?

- Is there any evidence of water intrusion or wood rot in the structural areas?
- Do any cracks indicate ongoing movement, or are they typical for the home's age?
- Is the crawlspace or basement properly ventilated and dry?
- Would you recommend a structural engineer for further evaluation?

How Arrow Home Inspections Supports You

Arrow Home Inspections will visually assess all accessible structural elements. We look for:

- Foundation integrity and moisture signs
- Structural framing issues in basements, crawlspaces, and attics
- Undersized, improperly installed, or deteriorated framing components
- Early signs of settlement, bowing, or failure

If deeper evaluation is needed, Arrow will suggest contacting a trusted:

- Structural engineer
- Foundation specialist
- Crawlspace and basement waterproofing contractor

- Wood rot remediation professional

Frequent Flyers on the Inspection Report

A home's structure is its backbone, and while the idea of "structural issues" may sound intimidating, many findings are simply signs of age, moisture exposure, or minor settling. Most are common in older homes and, once identified, can be stabilized or repaired with professional help. Inspections help you catch things early before they become major concerns.

Common Findings:

• Hairline Foundation Cracks – Usually caused by settling or shrinkage. Often cosmetic, but worth monitoring.

• Wood Framing Damage – Includes decay or insect damage in sills or beams.

• Uneven Floors – Can result from joist movement or minor settling. Common in older homes and often manageable.

• Cracked or Bowed Basement Walls – Often due to hydrostatic pressure.

• Rust on Structural Hardware – Minor surface rust is typical. Extensive rust may require cleaning or replacement.

Final Thought: Strong Bones Make a Safe Home

You can paint, patch, or update almost anything in a house—but if the bones aren't solid, you may be building on shaky ground. Arrow's structural review gives you the peace of mind to move forward—or the insight to negotiate repairs before you do.

Structural Elements Made Simple

Foundation: The base of a home, typically made from concrete, block, or stone, that supports the entire structure.

Efflorescence: A white, chalky residue on masonry walls caused by moisture drawing salts to the surface(often a sign of water intrusion).

Joists: Horizontal framing members that support floors or ceilings. They rest on beams or walls.

Beams: Load-bearing horizontal supports that span across open spaces and carry the weight of joists or the floor above.

Support Columns (or Posts): Vertical supports (metal, wood, or concrete) that carry weight from beams to the foundation or footings.

Framing: The wooden or metal skeleton of the home, including walls, floors, and roofs.

Settlement: The downward movement of the house caused by shifting or compacting soil beneath the foundation. May cause cracks or uneven floors.

Crawlspace: A shallow, unfinished space beneath the home used for access to plumbing or HVAC systems. Requires proper ventilation to avoid moisture issues.

Step Crack: A zigzag pattern of cracking in concrete block walls, often indicating foundation movement or stress.

Rim Joist: The outermost joist that caps the ends of floor joists. A common point of connection for decks and important for structural support.

Lally Column: A round, steel pipe filled with concrete, used as a permanent structural support under beams.

Screw Jack: A temporary adjustable metal post often used during construction; not typically rated for permanent load-bearing use.

Slab-on-Grade Foundation: A type of foundation where the home is built directly on a single, poured concrete slab. Common in ranch-style homes, it eliminates basements or crawl spaces. Plumbing and heating elements may be embedded in the slab, making access for repairs more difficult.

Truss Roof System: A prefabricated triangular framing structure that spans from one exterior wall to another, supporting the roof without requiring interior load-bearing walls. Allows for open floor plans and faster construction but must remain unmodified for structural integrity.

Radiant Slab Heating: A heating method where hot water tubing or electric heating elements are embedded within the concrete slab foundation. It delivers consistent, comfortable heat through the floor but can be costly and difficult to repair if leaks occur.

Explore Real-World Inspection Insights

Want to see what our inspectors actually find in the field? Visit our page for real photos and helpful context, organized by the same sections you've just read about. Whether you're buying, selling, or just curious, this gallery gives you a behind-the-scenes look at what we see or how to spot issues before they become problems.

Start exploring at Inspection Insights: arrow-homeinspections.com/inspection-insights or scan the QR code at the end of each chapter.

Structural Elements and Attic

Chapter Six

Attics and Framing

Don't Overlook the Overhead: Why Attics Matter More Than You Think

THE ATTIC IS ONE of the most overlooked spaces in a home, but it holds valuable clues about the home's condition, energy efficiency, and even structural integrity. Whether used for storage or simply as part of the home's thermal envelope, the attic plays a crucial role in ventilation, insulation, moisture control, and roof support.

Though not always fully accessible, what your inspector can see in the attic can reveal key insights about how well the home has been maintained and what may need attention.

A Brief Overview

Arrow Home Inspections evaluates all readily visible and accessible areas of the attic. This includes:

- Roof framing (rafters, trusses, or collar ties)
- Sheathing (roof deck boards)

- Insulation type and placement
- Ventilation systems and airflow
- Attic stairs or access points
- Visible wiring or exhaust vents from the home

Access is often limited due to insulation, finished surfaces, or tight entry points (like Scuttle, crawl hatches or pull-down stairs), but the inspection will highlight any issues that can be safely observed.

Why the Attic Matters

The attic may not be a living space, but it's where:

- Moisture problems often start
- Heat and cold enter or escape
- Roof structure weakness may first appear
- Mold, decay, or insulation gaps go unnoticed for years

A poorly maintained attic can impact energy bills, roof lifespan, and even air quality.

What Clients Should Understand

Roof Framing

- Watch for bowed wood, cracked rafters, or improper repairs; these can signal long-term roof stress or past damage.

- The framing in an attic typically consists of trusses, rafters, or collar ties. These structural members must be free of cracks, sagging, or signs of stress.

Attics: Look, But Don't Touch

Trusses

- In many homes the attic may reveal a truss roof system. These pre-engineered, triangular wooden structures span from one exterior wall to the other and carry the entire roof load.

- Because the weight is distributed through the trusses, no part of the system should ever be cut, notched, or drilled. Homeowners sometimes attempt to modify trusses to create more headroom or run HVAC or electrical lines, which can compromise the home's structural integrity.

Rafters and Stick Framing

- In contrast to trusses, traditional stick-built roof systems use individual rafters that slope from the ridge to the exterior walls. These systems often include collar ties or ceiling joists to prevent the walls from bowing outward under the weight of the roof. Unlike trusses, stick framing may allow for attic storage or finishing, but typically requires interior load-bearing walls.

Collar Ties

- These are horizontal framing members located in the upper third of the roof space, connecting opposing rafters. Their primary purpose is to resist outward thrust and roof uplift forces. Improper removal or damage to collar ties can compromise the roof structure and should be noted during inspection.

Roof Sheathing

- The sheathing (the wood boards or panels attached to the rafters) supports the roof shingles from below.
- Any sagging, staining, or soft spots may indicate leaks, past roof failures, or ongoing moisture problems.

Insulation

- Proper attic insulation helps regulate temperature, prevent ice dams, and reduce heating/cooling costs.
- Common types include blown-in cellulose, fiberglass batts, or spray foam.
- Insulation should be evenly distributed, not patchy, scattered, or missing in spots.
- Homes built before modern energy standards may have inadequate insulation, which should be evaluated and upgraded.
- Vermiculite insulation (particularly from the brand *Zonolite*) may contain asbestos and is sometimes found in older homes. If present, it should not be disturbed, and professional testing and abatement may be necessary.

Ventilation

- Good attic ventilation keeps air moving, preventing moisture buildup and overheating.
- Vents may be located at gable ends, soffits, ridge lines, or with powered attic fans.
- Poor ventilation can lead to mold, warped sheathing, or ice dams in winter.

Wiring and Exhaust Vents

- Any visible electrical conductors should be safely secured and protected from contact with insulation or framing.
- Bathroom or kitchen exhaust fans should never vent into the attic as they must discharge to the outside to prevent moisture accumulation and mold growth.

Wood-Destroying Insects in Attics

- Attics can sometimes show signs of wood-destroying insects, especially in older or poorly sealed homes. Arrow inspectors look for visible damage or exit holes that may indicate current or past activity.
- The four most common wood-destroying insects are:
    - Carpenter Bees – Bore into wood, often near eaves or exposed beams. Typically leave round holes.
    - Carpenter Ants – Nest in damp or decaying wood and can hollow out structural members.

  - Termites – Often difficult to detect. May leave mud tubes or damaged wood that sounds hollow.
  - Powder Post Beetles – Leave fine powdery dust (frass) and tiny exit holes. Activity is usually historic and dormant, but the damage remains visible.

Arrow documents these conditions and may recommend follow-up evaluation if signs are present.

What to Ask Your Inspector

- Is the roof framing in good condition with no signs of cracking or stress?
- Is the insulation adequate and evenly placed throughout the attic?
- Are there signs of moisture damage, staining, or poor ventilation?
- Are bathroom or dryer vents properly routed outside?
- Is the attic space safe and accessible for future maintenance or upgrades?
- Would you recommend adding or updating insulation or ventilation systems?

How Arrow Home Inspections Supports You

Arrow Home Inspections evaluates the attic with a focus on visible structural integrity, insulation condition, and ventilation performance. We assess:

- Cracked or damaged roof framing
- Inadequate or scattered insulation
- Moisture staining on sheathing or framing
- Signs of improper ventilation or vent discharge
- Unsafe or outdated electrical components (where visible)

If further investigation or upgrades are needed, Arrow may suggest you consult:

- Licensed insulation contractors
- Roofers or framing specialists
- Electricians for attic wiring
- Mold remediation or ventilation professionals

Frequent Flyers on the Inspection Report

Attics are like the unsung heroes of your home; they affect energy efficiency, ventilation, and even roof longevity. Many inspection issues here stem from poor airflow or old insulation. Luckily, most attic concerns are easy to address and don't spell disaster.

Common Findings:

• Missing or Disturbed Insulation – Gaps reduce energy efficiency. Blown-in or batt insulation can be added or adjusted.

• Blocked or Inadequate Ventilation – Soffit, ridge, or gable vents may be clogged or insufficient. Clearing and upgrading vents improves airflow and prevents mold.

• Improper Vent Discharge – Bathroom fans venting into the attic can cause moisture buildup. Should be redirected to the exterior.

• Damaged Sheathing or Rafters – Often due to leaks or past repairs. Spot fixes or reinforcement typically resolve it.

• Rodent or Pest Activity – Chewed wires or droppings may show past or current activity. Sealing gaps and pest control can mitigate issues.

Final Thought: Don't Skip the Space You Don't Use

You may never spend time in your attic, but what happens up there can affect the comfort, safety, and value of the entire home. From airflow and insulation to hidden roof problems, Arrow makes sure nothing important goes unnoticed even above the ceiling.

Attic & Roof Framing Terms Made Simple

Rafters: Sloped framing members that support the roof deck and transfer loads to exterior walls.

Trusses: Engineered triangular framing systems used in modern roofs for added strength and consistency.

Collar Ties: Horizontal members that connect opposing roof rafters near the peak, helping prevent roof spread.

Sheathing: The wood panels or boards attached to rafters or trusses to support roofing materials.

Blown-In Insulation: Loose-fill insulation (usually cellulose or fiberglass) applied by machine, to fill attic cavities or wall spaces. Ideal for covering irregular or hard-to-reach areas with even, consistent coverage.

Soffit Vents: Intake vents located under the roof eaves that allow fresh air into the attic.

Ridge Vent: A continuous vent at the roof's peak that allows hot air and moisture to escape the attic.

Gable Vent: A louvered vent on the gable end of a home, typically used for passive attic ventilation.

Ice Dams: Ridges of ice that form on the roof edge when attic heat melts snow, which refreezes over the soffit and can force water under shingles.

Vapor Barrier: A material or layer designed to slow the movement of moisture from warm interior air into cooler wall or roof cavities.

Attic Fan: A powered vent that helps expel hot or moist air from the attic space. Often controlled by a thermostat or humidistat.

Batt Insulation: Pre-cut sheets of insulation, typically made from fiberglass or mineral wool, designed to fit snugly between wall studs, attic joists, or floor beams. Common in attics.

Explore Real-World Inspection Insights

Want to see what our inspectors actually find in the field? Visit our page for real photos and helpful context, organized by the same sections you've just read about. Whether you're buying, selling, or just curious, this gallery gives you a behind-the-scenes look at what we see or how to spot issues before they become problems.

Start exploring at Inspection Insights: arrow-homeinspections.com/inspection-insights or scan the QR code at the end of each chapter.

Structural Elements and Attic

Chapter Seven

Behind the Bathroom Door

Small Room, Big Responsibilities

Bathrooms may be among the smallest rooms in the house, but they contain some of the most frequently used plumbing and ventilation systems. A typical home inspection will evaluate the visible fixtures and accessible plumbing to ensure everything is functioning as expected and to identify any signs of leaks, damage, or poor ventilation. Even small issues in a bathroom can quickly escalate into expensive water damage or mold problems if left unaddressed.

Why Bathrooms Matters

Because bathrooms combine moisture, electrical fixtures, and frequent use, problems here can create safety hazards, structural damage, or indoor air quality concerns. Poor drainage, improper ventilation, or worn-out caulking may not seem urgent but can lead to bigger headaches overtime.

What Clients Should Understand

- A slow-draining sink or tub could signal clogs or incorrect plumbing configurations.

- Flexible drain pipes (also called accordion or corrugated drains) are often a red flag, they clog easily and aren't generally code-compliant in many areas.

- Bathroom fans filled with lint or debris reduce airflow and can cause moisture buildup.

- Cracked or missing caulk around tubs or showers may allow for water to seep behind walls.

- Water stains or bubbling paint on the ceiling below a bathroom may suggest hidden leaks.

A Note on Plumbing Materials

Bathroom water supply and drainage systems are typically made from different materials depending on the home's age and any updates that have been made:

- Water Supply Lines: Most common materials include copper or PEX (cross-linked polyethylene). Both are durable, but PEX is more flexible andcommon in newer installations.

- Drain Lines: Drainage piping may be made from galvanized steel (older homes), copper, or PVC (polyvinyl chloride). Galvanized pipes may corrode internally over time, while PVC is the most common in modern construction and renovations.

Arrow inspectors note any visible signs of corrosion, outdated materials, or potential concerns related to these components.

What to Ask Your Inspector

- Are the sink, tub, and toilet fixtures draining properly?
- Is the bathroom ventilation adequate and vented to the outside?
- Is there evidence of active or previous water leaks?
- Are the plumbing materials used appropriate?
- Do you recommend having a licensed plumber evaluate any specific issues?

How Arrow HomeInspections Supports You

During a standard home inspection, Arrow visually evaluates the bathroom's fixtures, finishes,and plumbing access points to ensure they're safe and functional. This includes:

- Testing sinks, tubs, and toilets for visible leaks or slow drainage
- Checking the operation and condition of the exhaust fan
- Looking for signs of moisture intrusion in walls or flooring
- Noting damaged or missing caulk in wet areas
- Verifying GFCI protection for electrical outlets

If issues are found, we'll note whether they require a licensed plumber, electrician, or general contractor for further evaluation.

Frequent Flyers onthe Inspection Report

Bathrooms see a lot of daily use, so it's no surprise that wear and tear adds up. While leaks and moisture are common, most issues found in bathroom inspections are easy to remedy and usually cheaper to fix early before they cause bigger problems.

Common Findings:

• Slow Draining or Leaking Sinks or Tubs – SLOWDRAINS: Often caused by hair, soap scum, or buildup inside flexible drainpipes. LEAKS: Leaks are commonly found at connection points, under sink traps, or around old or improperly sealed fixtures. These issues are usually resolved by cleaning the drain, resealing joints, or replacing worn components.

• Loose or Inadequate Caulking – Gaps around tubs or showers can lead to water damage. Recaulking is a simple and effective solution.

• Ventilation Issues –Fans that vent into the attic or are clogged with debris need to be cleaned or redirected.

• Loose Toilets or Fixtures – Can cause leaks or rocking. Usually fixed with tightening or replacement of hardware.

• Minor Floor or Wall Damage – Moisture around the tub/shower can damage finishes. Most cosmetic issues are simple DIY repairs.

Final Thought: More Than Just Tile and Toilets

Bathrooms may be compact, but they require a lot of things to work correctly: plumbing, venting, waterproofing, and more. What seems like a minor defect could signal a larger maintenance issue, so never overlook this room during your inspection. Arrow helps you get straight to the point, so you know whether that pretty powder room is just a paint job or something more.

Bathroom Terms Made Simple

Accordion Drain / Flexible Drain Pipe: A ribbed, non-standard pipe commonly used under sinks. Prone to clogging and not ideal for permanent use.

Caulking: A waterproof sealant applied around tubs, sinks, or tile to prevent water intrusion.

GFCI (Ground Fault Circuit Interrupter): A safety outlet that shuts off power when moisture or electrical imbalance is detected. Required in bathrooms.

Shower Enclosure / Surround: The waterproof area surrounding a shower or tub, often made from tile, fiberglass, or acrylic.

Ventilation Fan: A ceiling-mounted fan that removes moisture and odors. It should vent to the exterior, not into the attic.

Copper Pipe: A durable metal piping material used for water supply lines, known for reliability and long lifespan.

PEX: A flexible plastic tubing commonly used in modern plumbing systems for water supply lines.

Galvanized Steel: Steel pipe coated with zinc to prevent rusting, commonly used for drain lines in older homes but prone to internal corrosion.

PVC: Lightweight plastic piping widely used for drain and vent lines in modern homes due to ease of installation and resistance to corrosion.

Explore Real-World Inspection Insights

Want to see what our inspectors actually find in the field? Visit our page for real photos and helpful context, organized by the same sections you've just read about. Whether you're buying, selling, or just curious, this gallery gives you a behind-the-scenes look at what we see or how to spot issues before they become problems.

Start exploring at Inspection Insights: arrow-homeinspections.com/inspection-insights or scan the QR code at the end of each chapter.

Bathrooms and Kitchens

Chapter Eight

Kitchens

The Heart of the Home, Inspected

The kitchen is often called the heart of the home and for good reason. It's where we cook, gather, and sometimes even work or do homework. But from an inspection standpoint, the kitchen is also packed with appliances, plumbing, electrical systems, and built-in elements that all need to function properly for the space to be safe, clean, and fully usable.

During a kitchen inspection, Arrow Home Inspections focuses on the built-in elements of the kitchen, not personal appliances. We test fixtures and evaluate any permanently installed components to identify functional issues, safety concerns, or signs of wear.

What's Checked During a Kitchen Inspection

- Range, oven, or cooktop (gas or electric)

- Ventilation equipment or range hood

- Built-in dishwasher

• Garbage disposal (if present)

• Sink and visible plumbing

• GFCI-protected electrical outlets

• Cabinets, drawers, and countertops

• Flooring, walls, and ceiling conditions

Why Kitchens Matter

Your kitchen isn't just about convenience, it's a high-traffic zone with multiple systems that must work together safely. A poorly vented stove, a malfunctioning GFCI outlet, or a leaking sink can lead to:

• Water damage and mold beneath cabinets

• Fire or electrical hazards

• Inoperable appliances that require costly repairs

• Safety concerns, especially if ventilation is compromised

• Disruption to daily life if not addressed

What Clients Should Understand

Range & Oven

- Whether electric or gas, we test the main functions of the range and oven.

- Common issues include broken knobs, failing igniters, or non-functioning burners.
- Gas ranges must be properly vented and should not emit a gas odor when off.

Ventilation (Range Hood)

- Kitchen ventilation is either ducted (vented outdoors) or recirculating (filters air and recirculates it).
- Recirculating fans must have clean, properly installed filters.
- Poor ventilation can lead to grease buildup and poor air quality.

Sink & Plumbing

- We check for leaks under the sink, run the faucet, and inspect drainage.
- Loose fixtures, dripping faucets, or slow drains may be noted.
- Leaks in this area can cause mold or wood decay inside cabinetry.

Dishwasher

- We run a short cycle to ensure the unit turns on and drains properly.
- Older dishwashers may still function but show signs of wear or age.

- Signs of rust, leaks, or door seal failure are common concerns.

GFCI Outlets

- GFCI (Ground Fault Circuit Interrupter) outlets are required within six feet of a water source.
- We test GFCIs to ensure they trip and reset properly.
- Missing GFCIs or non-functioning outlets are common red flags.

Cabinets, Counters & Floors

- We assess doors, drawers, and shelves for alignment and function.
- Loose laminate, chipped counters, or cracked tiles may be noted.
- Warping, sagging, or decay (especially near water sources) may indicate prior leaks.

What to Ask Your Inspector

- Do all appliances turn on and function safely?
- Is the kitchen properly ventilated for the type of cooking appliance?
- Are any water leaks or plumbing issues visible beneath the sink?
- Are GFCI outlets installed and working near water sources?
- Do any areas show signs of water damage, decay, or previous leaks?

• Would you recommend servicing or replacing any appliances?

How Arrow Home Inspections Supports You

Arrow Home Inspections provides a full visual review of the kitchen during every home inspection, including:

• Running built-in appliances through a basic function test

• Testing electrical outlets and GFCIs

• Checking sinks, faucets, and under-sink plumbing

• Observing for cabinet or flooring damage due to leaks

• Calling out visible wear, safety issues, or missing components

If any appliance or system is inoperable, we'll document it clearly and recommend:

• Servicing by a licensed technician

• Specialist review of older or damaged appliances

• Replacement planning if a system is nearing the end of its life

Frequent Flyers on the Inspection Report

Kitchens are one of the most used spaces in a home and also one of the most inspected. Many of the issues we uncover are age-related or wear-related, not deal-breakers. The goal is to know what works, what's nearing the end of its life, and what might need a little extra attention.

Common Findings:

• Non-Functioning Range Burners or Knobs – Often due to wear or user damage; replacement parts are available.

• Loose Ventilation Hoods – A simple repair, but unsecured fans can rattle, fail to filter properly, or even fall.

• Leaking Under-Sink Plumbing – A frequent issue; may be caused by loose fittings or degraded seals.

• Outdated or Missing GFCI Outlets – Easily upgraded to meet current safety codes.

• Dishwasher Wear or Leaks – Often due to age; a fair rating means the appliance works but may be nearing replacement.

Final Thought: The Kitchen Doesn't Lie

If something's not working, you'll likely notice fast. That's why kitchen inspections matter because every squeaky cabinet, leaky faucet, or shorted outlet tells a story. Arrow Home Inspections helps you listen before you buy.

Kitchen Terms Made Simple

GFCI Outlet: A Ground Fault Circuit Interrupter outlet that shuts off power when it detects a ground fault. Required near sinks and other wet areas for safety.

Recirculating Vent: A kitchen range hood that filters and recirculates air instead of venting it outside. Common in condos and older homes.

Range Hood: A ventilation device above the stove that removes smoke, steam, and cooking odors. Can be vented outside or recirculating.

Dishwasher: A built-in appliance that uses water jets and detergent to clean dishes. Inspected for leaks, drainage, and function.

Garbage Disposal: An under-sink device that grinds food waste so it can pass through plumbing. Not always present.

Base Cabinet: The lower section of cabinetry that sits directly on the floor and supports countertops.

Wall Cabinet: Cabinets mounted above the counter or appliances, used for upper-level storage.

Laminate Countertop: A synthetic surface commonly used in kitchens. Affordable, but prone to chipping or peeling.

Undermount Sink: A sink installed beneath the countertop surface. Requires proper sealing to prevent water damage.

Anti-Tip Bracket: A small device that secures a range or stove to the floor or wall to prevent tipping; often required by code.

Explore Real-World Inspection Insights

Want to see what our inspectors actually find in the field? Visit our page for real photos and helpful context, organized by the same sections you've just read about. Whether you're buying, selling, or just curious, this gallery gives you a behind-the-scenes look at what we see or how to spot issues before they become problems.

Start exploring at Inspection Insights: arrow-homeinspections.com/inspection-insights or scan the QR code at the end of each chapter.

Bathrooms and Kitchens

Chapter Nine

Interior Elements

What Lies Beneath (and Above and Beside)

INTERIOR ELEMENTS GIVE YOUR home its personality, but they also serve a structural and safety purpose. From walls and ceilings to windows and floors, the inspection of interior components focuses on what's visible and accessible. The goal isn't to critique design or aesthetics, but to identify areas that may indicate underlying damage, moisture intrusion, improper installation, or wear that could affect habitability or future costs.

Arrow Home Inspections assesses interior walls, ceilings, stairs, railings, doors, and windows to check for function, safety, and visible signs of damage. Garage doors, steps, and installed hardware are also included.

Why Interior Elements Matter

These elements contribute to both safety and comfort. A properly functioning window doesn't just provide light; it also provides ventilation and emergency egress. A solid floor isn't just for looks, it prevents trip hazards and costly repairs.

Key areas assessed:

* Doors (fit, function, locks, hardware)

* Windows (open/close function, screens, visible damage)

* Walls and ceilings (cracks, staining, moisture indicators)

* Stairs and railings (spacing, strength, trip hazards)

* Garage doors (auto-reverse sensors, physical condition, opener function)

What Buyers Should Understand

A few paint chips or worn floors are normal, but these may also hint at deeper issues. Common interior findings include:

* Blown Thermal Seals: Blown thermal panes can cause windows (and glass doors) to appear foggy or streaked. While not urgent, as they reduce visibility and may indicate aging materials, they do not affect energy efficiency.

* Non-functional lights or outlets: May indicate a simple bulb or a deeper wiring issue. If it's unclear, a licensed electrician should evaluate.

* Damaged window screens or missing locks: Typically low-cost fixes, but they affect security and ventilation.

* Cracks in drywall or plaster: Can be cosmetic, but larger or angled cracks may signal settling or structural movement.

* Stairs without center stringers or uneven risers: Common in older homes and easy to upgrade for safety. Loose or missing railings and notes any balusters spaced more than 4 inches apart, a common safety hazard, especially for children. Railings are typically required on open sides of staircases for proper support and fall prevention.

What to Ask Your Inspector

* Are there any cracks that might indicate structural movement?

* Are stairs and railings secure and up to code?

* Do windows open, close, and lock properly?

* Is there any indication of past water damage or staining?

* Do garage door sensors and openers work correctly?

How Arrow Home Inspections Supports You

Arrow looks beyond the surface to identify functional and safety concerns, including:

* Window operation and condition

* Door fit, latch, and security

* Visible signs of moisture or staining

* Stair safety, spacing, and railing stability

* Garage door functionality and sensor alignment

We don't evaluate paint colors or carpet choices—but we do identify red flags that could cost you later.

Frequent Flyers on the Inspection Report

Interior issues are often cosmetic, but that doesn't mean they should be ignored. These common findings pop up often and are almost always manageable with basic repair, replacement, or maintenance. Small interior issues may indicate bigger patterns over time, so catching them early helps you plan and budget with confidence.

Common Findings:

* Fogged or Broken Window/Door Seals: These failed seals reduce visibility due to trapped moisture between panes but have minimal impact on energy efficiency. Resolution typically involves replacing the insulated glass unit.

* Non-Working Lights or Outlets: Sometimes due to bulbs, but can also point to loose wiring or older fixtures.

* Stair or Railing Issues: Loose, improperly spaced, or missing handrails are common and typically inexpensive to fix.

* Ceiling Stains or Cracks: May indicate past leaks or minor settling. Always worth asking if the cause was addressed.

* Warped or Worn Flooring: From water damage, heavy furniture, or age—often cosmetic but can hide subfloor issues.

Final Thought: More Than Meets the Eye

Interior elements may seem simple, but they offer valuable clues about a home's age, use, and care. Don't overlook a sticky door or cracked wall, they may tell a deeper story. Arrow Home Inspections gets you straight to the point with a functional review of the spaces you live in every day.

Interior Elements Made Simple

Blown Thermal Seal (Windows and Doors): A failure in the seal between panes of double- or triple-pane windows/doors, allowing moisture to enter the space between the panes. This often results in fogging, condensation, or a cloudy appearance that cannot be cleaned from the inside or outside. While not usually a structural concern, it affects energy efficiency and visibility.

Railing: A safety barrier along stairs or balconies. Proper height and secure attachment are essential for safety.

Center Stringer: A middle structural support under a stairway. Adds strength and reduces bounce in wider stairs.

Warped Flooring: When floorboards bend or lift, often due to moisture or improper installation.

Settling Crack: A minor crack in walls or ceilings caused by normal foundation movement. Usually cosmetic but worth monitoring.

Garage Door Sensor: A required safety feature that uses an infrared beam to detect obstructions (people, pets, etc); if triggered, it stops and reverses the door to prevent injury or damage.

Sheetrock: Also known as drywall. A common wall material made from gypsum board.

Double-Hung Window: A window with two movable sashes that slide vertically. Allows for better airflow.

Egress Window: A window large enough and positioned properly to be used as an emergency exit (IRC Section R310). For above-grade bedrooms, the window must provide a net clear opening of at least 5.7 square feet, with a minimum height of 24 inches, minimum width of 20 inches, and a sill height no more than 44 inches from the floor. It must be operable from the inside without tools, keys, or special knowledge. In basement bedrooms, the same size requirements apply, but if the window is below grade, a window well must be at least 36 inches wide and extend 36 inches out from the wall. If the window well is deeper than 44 inches, a permanently affixed ladder or steps must be present for safe egress.

Baseboard: The trim along the bottom of interior walls, hiding gaps and protecting from scuffs.

Explore Real-World Inspection Insights

Want to see what our inspectors actually find in the field? Visit our page for real photos and helpful context, organized by the same sections you’ve just read about. Whether you're buying, selling, or just curious, this gallery gives you a behind-the-scenes look at what we see or how to spot issues before they become problems.

Start exploring at Inspection Insights: arrow-homeinspections.com/inspection-insights or scan the QR code at the end of each chapter.

Interior Elements

Chapter Ten

Foundation and Substructure

From the Ground Down

YOUR FOUNDATION IS MORE than just a structural base, it supports the entire home and protects it from moisture, settling, and ground movement. In New England homes, you'll see a variety of foundation types depending on the age and construction style of the property. Each type has unique maintenance needs, typical signs of wear, and inspection considerations.

Arrow Home Inspections evaluates the visible and accessible areas of the foundation and substructure. Finished basements and walls may limit full visibility, but your inspector will always assess exposed sections and note any signs of moisture intrusion, material failure, or structural concern.

Common Foundation Types in the Northeast:

- Fieldstone: Found in older and/or historic homes. These

require frequent pointing and are more susceptible to water penetration.

- Poured Concrete: Common in modern homes. Durable, but prone to cracking due to settlement or hydrostatic pressure.
- Concrete Block (Cinder Block): Easy to install and strong. May develop step-cracks along mortar joints if settling occurs.
- Brick: Typically used in older or decorative structures. Susceptible to mortar erosion over time.
- Granite: Seen in older or upscale properties. Very durable but still vulnerable at joints.
- Slab-on-Grade: A flat concrete slab poured at ground level. No basement or crawlspace; limited access to plumbing and insulation. Can crack from soil movement or moisture fluctuations.

Substructure elements include beams, joists, support columns, floor slabs, and the basement stairs. In older homes, a mix of wood and metal may be used. Your inspector will check for sagging, decay, rust, or signs of movement where possible.

Why the Foundation and Substructure Matter

These foundation and substructure:

- Provide structural stability and load distribution

- Help resist shifting due to soil conditions or moisture
- Play a role in managing basement moisture and airflow
- Contribute to the home's long-term durability and safety

Unstable foundations can cause uneven floors, cracked walls, sticking doors, and even major structural compromise if left unaddressed. Early detection is key.

What Clients Should Understand

While full foundation inspections may be limited in finished basements, Arrow Home Inspections will:

- Evaluate accessible exposed walls for cracking, bowing, moisture stains, or efflorescence
- Note any movement, separation, or gaps in structural beams and posts
- Look for spalling, cracking, or crumbling concrete, settling or deteriorating brick and mortar
- Observe visible subfloor framing for signs of decay or pest activity, or wood-destroying Insects (WDI's)
- Look for evidence of rodents or wood-destroying insects

If potential concerns are noted, Arrow will recommend follow-up with licensed professionals who specialize in foundation repair or structural engineering.

Wood-Destroying Insects: What to Watch For

Foundations and substructures often show the first visible signs of activity from wood-destroying insects (WDIs). Arrow inspectors are trained to identify common red flags associated with the four most common species:

- Termites – These insects can cause significant structural damage by feeding on wood from the inside out. Look for mud tubes, hollow-sounding beams, or damaged subfloor framing near the foundation.

- Carpenter Ants – Attracted to moist or decaying wood, these ants hollow out galleries for nesting, especially near sill plates or damp corners of the foundation.

- Carpenter Bees – Often mistaken for bumblebees, they drill round holes into exposed wood, typically overhangs or structural framing near the basement bulkhead or walkout.

- Powder post Beetles – These beetles leave behind fine, talc-like powder and tiny exit holes in exposed wood. While most infestations are inactive or dormant, visible damage should still be noted.

Arrow will comment on visible evidence of past or present WDI activity and may recommend further evaluation or treatment by a licensed pest control specialist, particularly in areas with structural framing exposed at the basement level.

What to Ask Your Inspector

When reviewing the foundation and substructure of a home, consider asking:

- Are there visible cracks, moisture stains, or signs of movement in the foundation walls?
- Can you determine the type of foundation and its typical maintenance needs?
- Are the support beams and columns in good condition?
- Are there any signs of sagging, shifting, or pest activity (WDI's) in the subfloor or joists?
- Does the basement layout or finishing limit your ability to inspect key structural elements?

How Arrow Home Inspections Supports You

When you schedule an inspection with Arrow, you're getting more than just a glance at the surface. Even when finished materials limit visibility, our inspectors are trained to identify telltale signs of underlying foundation or substructure concerns often using tools like a thermal imaging camera and communicate their findings clearly. Arrow Home Inspections provides:

- A thorough evaluation of visible foundation walls, floor slabs, and support structures

- Professional documentation of any cracks, moisture signs, sagging, or material deterioration
- Insight into the type of foundation present and what that means for future upkeep
- Observations about structural beams, joists, and piers that are accessible at the time of inspection
- Guidance on whether any follow-up evaluation by a licensed structural expert or foundation specialist is warranted
- Digital resources and videos to help homeowners better understand what common issues may look like and how to address them

Frequent Flyers on the Inspection Report

Foundations are designed to last but that doesn't mean they're immune to wear, weather, or time. In New England, where soil conditions and older housing stock present unique challenges, foundation concerns are common. The good news? Most are manageable and don't necessarily indicate major failure.

Common Findings:

- Hairline Foundation Cracks: Often caused by normal settlement or shrinkage; easily sealed and monitored.
- Efflorescence: White powdery substance on walls caused by water vapor; often just cosmetic, but a sign to check drainage.

- Bowed or Bulging Walls: Indicates lateral pressure from soil; may require reinforcement or bracing.
- Rusted Lally Columns and Decaying Wood Posts: Lally: Steel support posts that can rust or corrode, especially at the base. Wood Posts: Vertical structural supports made of lumber; vulnerable to rot, insect damage, or warping if exposed to moisture or improper footing, and should be monitored for decay or instability. Typically found in older homes and replaceable with modern alternatives.
- Moisture Intrusion: Signs of water stains, musty odors, or puddles; usually improved with gutters, grading, or a sump pump.

Final Thought: Foundation First, Worry Later

Most foundation issues aren't emergencies. The key is identifying them early, understanding the cause, and working with professionals to keep things stable. When Arrow Home Inspections evaluates your home's substructure, you're getting a down-to-earth perspective that helps you move forward with confidence.

Foundations and Substructure Terms Made Simple

Fieldstone: Rounded natural stones used in older foundations, held together with mortar. Requires regular upkeep.

Poured Concrete: A continuous concrete wall formed using molds. Durable but may crack with pressure or time.

Concrete Block: Also known as cinder block. Hollow rectangular units stacked and mortared into place.

Brick: Traditional bricks are made from natural clay that is molded and fired in a kiln to harden. This process creates fired clay bricks, which are durable, weather-resistant, and commonly used in older or decorative foundations. While strong, the mortar joints between them can wear down over time and may require repointing.

Granite: Hard, natural stone often used in upscale or historic foundations. Strong, but seams can fail.

Efflorescence: White, chalky residue left behind when moisture evaporates from masonry surfaces. It indicates moisture intrusion or migration through the wall, often due to poor drainage or waterproofing.

Lally Column: Steel support posts used to hold up beams. Often found in basements.

Beam: A horizontal structural element that supports the floor joists.

Joist: A structural member used to support a floor or ceiling, typically made of wood.

Subfloor: The layer beneath finished flooring, supported by joists.

Slab: A poured concrete floor commonly found in basements or garages.

Settlement: The natural downward movement of a foundation as the soil beneath it adjusts.

Carpenter Ants: Large ants that tunnel through moist wood to build nests, weakening structural components over time.

Carpenter Bees: Solitary bees that bore round holes into exposed wood surfaces, often found under eaves or trim.

Powderpost Beetles: Wood-boring beetles that leave behind fine powder and pin-sized exit holes; often found in older homes, mostly dormant.

Termites: Insects that consume wood and can cause serious structural damage; typically detected via mud tubes or hollow-sounding wood.

Explore Real-World Inspection Insights

Want to see what our inspectors actually find in the field? Visit our page for real photos and helpful context, organized by the same sections you've just read about. Whether you're buying, selling, or just curious, this gallery gives you a behind-the-scenes look at what we see or how to spot issues before they become problems.

Start exploring at Inspection Insights: arrow-homeinspections.com/inspection-insights or scan the QR code at the end of each chapter.

Foundation Substructure and Water Penetration

Chapter Eleven

Foundation Area Water Penetration

Where Moisture Comes In and How to Keep It Out

WATER IS ONE OF the most common culprits behind home maintenance headaches. Whether it seeps in from the soil, trickles in through a crack, or builds up from poor drainage, moisture can lead to mold, structural damage, and costly repairs. That's why water penetration in the foundation area deserves serious attention during a home inspection.

Arrow Home Inspections evaluates both the exterior and interior signs of water intrusion at or below grade level, where basements and foundations are most vulnerable. This includes visible indicators like staining, musty odors, high humidity, cracks, and pooling water. While inspectors may be limited to what is visible at the time of inspection (due to factors like finished basements, stored belongings, or wall coverings) they use tools such as moisture meters and thermal imaging cameras, along with a trained eye, to identify telltale signs of hidden issues.

Common Sources of Foundation Water Penetration:

- Poor site grading
- Missing or short downspout extensions
- Faulty or undersized gutters
- Cracked foundation walls or slabs
- Inadequate or failed sump pumps

Why It Matters

Persistent water penetration can:

- Promote mold growth and air quality issues
- Deteriorate wood framing and subfloors
- Attract pests like termites or rodents
- Weaken foundation materials over time
- Lower property value and make resale more difficult

What Clients Should Understand

Water penetration is extremely common in New England homes, especially those with basements. The good news? Most causes are manageable, and with the right improvements, water issues can be resolved or significantly minimized.

Your inspection report may include:

- Visual signs of current or prior water intrusion (e.g., staining, bubbling paint, musty smell)
- Observations of sump pump functionality and placement
- Notations on exterior drainage conditions
- Recommendations to consult a specialist if chronic issues are suspected

It's also important to know that a dry basement during your inspection doesn't always guarantee a water-tight future. Talk to your Agent to see if asking the seller for disclosures and history related to past water issues is appropriate or available.

What to Ask Your Inspector

When reviewing the foundation area for water intrusion, consider asking:

- Are there signs of past or active moisture intrusion in the basement or crawlspace?
- Does the grading or drainage system appear sufficient to direct water away from the home?
- Is there a sump pump present, and does it appear functional?

- Are there visible signs of efflorescence (a white, powdery substance that forms on masonry, concrete, or brick surfaces when water seeps through and evaporates, leaving behind salt deposits. While usually harmless, it can signal moisture intrusion that may warrant further investigation), staining, or musty odors that may indicate water issues?
- Would you recommend any further evaluation by a water-proofing specialist or structural engineer?

How Arrow Home Inspections Supports You

Your standard inspection will include:

- Exterior grading and drainage evaluation near the foundation
- Visual check for staining, efflorescence, or moisture damage inside basement walls
- Assessment of sump pump and french drain placement (if present)
- Recommendations for improving water management
- Clear documentation with photos and easy-to-understand explanations

Frequent Flyers on the Inspection Report

Basement and crawlspace moisture is one of the most frequent concerns in real estate inspections and for good reason. Water damage can hide behind walls, under carpets, or even inside concrete. Fortunately, many solutions are simple, and catching issues early can save you thousands.

Common Findings:

- Improper Downspout Discharge: Water too close to the foundation; extensions solve the problem.
- Negative Grading Near Foundation: Soil slopes toward home; resolved with soil regrading.
- Efflorescence on Walls: White powdery residue from water movement; cosmetic but worth noting.
- Nonfunctional or Poorly Placed Sump Pump: Pump too close to electrical panels or not connected to an exterior drain.
- Staining or Peeling Paint in Finished Areas: Often signs of historical water intrusion.

Final Thought: Moisture Happens, Management Matters

A little moisture doesn't mean a big problem—but ignoring it might. Arrow Home Inspections helps you identify vulnerabilities and suggests practical next steps, giving you peace of mind and a clear path forward.

Foundation Area Water Penetration Terms

Efflorescence: A white, chalky substance left on masonry surfaces when water evaporates and leaves salt deposits behind.

Sump Pump: A device used to remove water from a basement or crawlspace, usually installed in a pit below floor level.

Grading: The slope of the ground around a home. Positive grading moves water away from the foundation; negative grading brings it toward the structure.

Downspout Extension: A pipe or flexible hose that attaches to the bottom of a gutter downspout to direct water farther from the home's base.

Hydrostatic Pressure: Pressure from groundwater that builds up and pushes against basement slab, walls, or floors. Can cause cracks, leaks, or structural stress.

French Drain: A system of perforated piping placed around the perimeter of the foundation, installed underground to collect and redirect water away from the home typically discharging to a dry well or a safe area of the yard graded away from the structure.

Vapor Barrier: A material, often plastic or foil, used to slow or stop moisture from moving into a building, typically installed in crawl-spaces or behind walls.

Moisture Intrusion: The unwanted entry of water or vapor into a building component, often leading to damage or mold.

Waterproofing Membrane: A specialized coating or layer applied to foundation walls or basement floors to prevent water seepage.

Dehumidifier: A household appliance that removes excess moisture from the air, reducing humidity levels and helping to prevent mold growth.

Explore Real-World Inspection Insights

Want to see what our inspectors actually find in the field? Visit our page for real photos and helpful context, organized by the same sections you've just read about. Whether you're buying, selling, or just curious, this gallery gives you a behind-the-scenes look at what we see or how to spot issues before they become problems.

Start exploring at Inspection Insights: arrow-homeinspections.com/inspection-insights or scan the QR code at the end of each chapter.

Foundation Substructure and Water Penetration

Chapter Twelve

Heating Systems and Air-Conditioning

Staying Warm or Cool: What's Fueling Your Comfort

WHETHER YOU'RE STEPPING INTO a charming 1900s colonial or a modern townhouse, understanding the heating and air-conditioning systems are essential. In New England homes, heating systems can vary widely in age, fuel type, and distribution method. The two most common built-in air conditioning systems in the Northeast are ducted central air and ductless mini-splits. Ducted systems are typically found in newer homes or those with existing forced-air heating (like gas or oil furnaces), while mini-splits are increasingly popular in older homes without ductwork because they're easier to install and provide energy-efficient, targeted heating and cooling. During the inspection, Arrow Home Inspections examines all accessible components of the heating system and AC system, identifies its energy source, notes its condition, and offers insights into long-term maintenance.

Why Heating and Cooling Systems Matter

A properly functioning system isn't just about comfort, it's about safety, efficiency, and longevity. These systems affect:

- Monthly energy costs
- Indoor air quality and moisture levels
- Structural integrity (e.g., frozen pipes from insufficient heat)
- Carbon monoxide safety (for fuel-based systems)
- Year-round climate control and resale appeal

Regular maintenance and early detection of minor issues help extend system lifespan and prevent costly repairs.

What Clients Should Understand

Arrow inspectors help clients make sense of the wide variety of systems found in the region:

- Fuel Types: Natural gas, oil, propane, and also electric. Each has pros and cons in cost, efficiency, and availability.
- System Age & Life Expectancy:
    - Furnaces and boilers: 20–25 years
    - Central air conditioning: 15–20 years
    - Mini-splits: 15–20 years with proper maintenance

- Heat Distribution Systems: Common heating methods in the Northeast include forced hot air, hydronic baseboards, radiant floor systems, and steam radiators (* see spotlight below), each delivering warmth differently depending on the home's age and infrastructure.

- Cooling Distribution Systems: Cooling is typically provided by central air systems using ductwork or ductless mini-split systems, especially in homes without existing ducts.

- Thermostat Controls: Can be central or zoned, programmable or smart.

- Radiant (In-Floor) Heating: Found in some mid-century homes and high-efficiency renovations, this system delivers heat through tubing embedded in floors—usually concrete slabs. It offers even warmth and energy efficiency but can be difficult and expensive to repair if issues arise beneath the surface.

- Gravity Heating Systems: Typically found in very old homes, these systems rely on natural convection (hot air rising, cool air falling) rather than fans or pumps. They often use large ducts and massive furnaces. While uncommon today, some remain functional. Arrow evaluates whether these legacy systems are safe and recommends modern upgrades when needed.

A system may "work" during an inspection, but subtle signs like rust, smells, or odd noises may warrant further evaluation.

*** Spotlight on Heat: Steam Systems**

Steam heat is not common in modern construction, but it's a charming and historically significant system that still exists in many older New England homes, especially pre-1950 properties. At Arrow Home Inspections, we love highlighting these legacy systems for the education they offer and the unique care they require.

How Steam Systems Work:
Steam systems heat water in a boiler until it turns into steam. That steam travels through pipes and into large cast iron radiators located throughout the home. These systems provide consistent, radiant warmth that many homeowners find deeply comfortable in colder months.

Key Features & Inspection Points:

- Radiators: These are often large, heavy units, sometimes with ornate designs. They retain heat well but can be uneven in distribution across rooms.
- Balancing & Maintenance: Older systems can be tricky to balance. Look for signs like spitting valves, uneven heating, hissing noises, or water stains around radiators.
- Sight Glass: A vertical glass tube on the boiler allows you to monitor the water level. Maintaining the proper water level is crucial for safe and efficient operation.
- Manual Refills vs. Auto-Feeders:
    - Many systems require manual refilling by opening a valve to add water.

    - More modernized setups may include an automatic water feeder, but even those require occasional monitoring to ensure proper function.

- Sediment & Pressure: Periodic draining helps remove sediment that builds up inside the boiler. Homeowners must also watch pressure gauges to avoid over-pressurization or shutdowns.

Why It's Worth Noting:
While not commonly installed in today's homes, steam systems offer a window into how heating has evolved. They also present a different kind of maintenance routine—one that demands attentiveness but can deliver cozy, efficient warmth when properly cared for.

Mini-Splits: Room-by-Room Comfort

Mini-split or ductless systems provide zoned heating and cooling, ideal for homes without ductwork or for add-ons. They include:

- Indoor wall-mounted air handlers
- Outdoor compressor unit
- Remote or smart thermostat control

Arrow checks for proper installation, drain line integrity, and visible signs of wear or improper slope.

HVAC vs. Furnace vs. Boiler: What's the Difference?

Boiler

- **What it does:** Heats water for radiators or baseboard heating
- **Fuel type:** Gas or oil
- **Offers AC?** No
- **Common in:** Older homes without ductwork

Furnace

- **What it does:** Heats air and distributes it through ducts
- **Fuel type:** Gas, oil, or electric
- **Offers AC?** Yes, if paired with a central AC system
- **Common in:** Homes with ductwork

HVAC (Heating, Ventilation & Air Conditioning)

- **What it does:** Provides integrated heating and cooling
- **Fuel type:** Gas, electric, or heat pump
- **Offers AC?** Yes
- **Common in:** Newer or recently remodeled homes

Arrow inspects your setup and highlights any signs of deferred maintenance or outdated systems.

Air Conditioning: Cool Heads Prevail

Air conditioning can be central (via ducts), ductless (mini-splits), or portable. Arrow focuses on:

- System Type: Central AC and mini-splits
- Condenser Unit: Checked for level placement, damage, debris, and clear airflow
- Thermostat: Functionality and correct placement
- Age and Noise: Older units may still cool but could be inefficient or loud

Note: AC systems are not operated during cold weather (<60°F) to prevent damage.

What to Ask Your Inspector

- What type of system do I have, and how old is it?
- Is the fuel type common or expensive to maintain?
- Are there safety concerns, such as rust or improper venting?
- Are heating and cooling evenly distributed?
- Are there signs that the system has been maintained?

How Arrow Home Inspections Supports You

Arrow's role is to give you clarity, not confusion. We help clients understand:

- The system type and energy source
- Any red flags; rust, corrosion, leaks, poor venting
- Functional thermostats and emergency shut-off switches
- System age, visible maintenance, and general condition
- Mini-split functionality and condenser condition
- When to call a licensed HVAC tech, plumber, or electrician

Frequent Flyers on the Inspection Report: Heating & Cooling

The systems that keep your home comfortable are often hidden—and frequently overlooked until something breaks. Arrow helps you spot common heating and cooling red flags before they become costly surprises.

Common Findings:

- Corroded Boiler Pipes or Heat Exchangers: Rust, mineral buildup, or pinhole leaks can reduce efficiency and lead to major failures over time.
- Thermostat Issues: Detached, unresponsive, or outdated thermostats can affect comfort and system performance.

Many older units lack programmable features or zoning support.

- Venting and Exhaust Problems: Blocked or improperly pitched flue pipes, missing draft hoods, or backdrafting can pose serious safety risks (especially with gas or oil systems).
- Missing or Unlabeled Shut-Offs: Especially in older homes, heating components may lack clearly marked or accessible shut-off valves, complicating emergency response or maintenance.
- Leaking Mini-Split Refrigerant Lines or Drainage Issues: Improperly installed or aging mini-split systems may show signs of condensate leaks or loss of refrigerant, which reduces cooling and may damage interior walls.
- Cooling Failure in Aged Systems: Central AC units or mini-splits beyond 10–15 years may no longer cool effectively. Arrow checks for temperature differentials and overall condition.

Final Thought: Keep It Cool, Keep It Cozy

Heating and cooling are basic needs, but they're not basic systems. Understanding your setup helps you stay warm in February and cool in July. Arrow Home Inspections gets you straight to the point, so you're never left in the dark.

Heating and Cooling Terms Made Simple

Boiler: Heats water for baseboard or radiators. Common in older homes.

Furnace: Heats air and distributes it via ducts. Often paired with central AC.

HVAC: Combined system providing heating, ventilation, and air conditioning.

Mini-Split: Ductless system providing heating and cooling to individual rooms.

Radiant Heat: Heating through floors using hot water or electric coils.

Baseboard Heat: Hot water heating element mounted at the base of walls.

Steam Radiator: Cast iron radiator emitting steam heat.

Thermostat: Temperature control device; may be programmable or smart.

Condenser Unit and Air Handler: The air handler is the indoor unit that distributes air throughout your home. The condenser unit is the outdoor component that removes heat from the indoor air. Together, they form a complete central air conditioning system.

Emergency Shut-Off Switch: Required kill switch for heating systems, usually at top of basement stairs.

Venting System: Exhaust system allowing combustion gases to escape safely.

Circulator Pump: Moves hot water through a boiler system.

Fuel Source: Type of energy used; gas, oil, electric, or propane.

Heat Exchanger: Transfers heat within furnaces; cracks or rust can be hazardous.

Explore Real-World Inspection Insights

Want to see what our inspectors actually find in the field? Visit our page for real photos and helpful context, organized by the same sections you've just read about. Whether you're buying, selling, or just curious, this gallery gives you a behind-the-scenes look at what we see or how to spot issues before they become problems.

Start exploring at Inspection Insights: arrow-homeinspections.com/inspection-insights or scan the QR code at the end of each chapter.

Heat (AC) and Hot Water

Chapter Thirteen

Hot Water

The Unsung Hero of Modern Comfort

HOT WATER IS SOMETHING most of us take for granted, until we don't have it. Whether it's an invigorating morning shower or running the dishwasher after dinner, the hot water system in your home plays a critical role in daily life. Arrow Home Inspections checks the function, installation, and general condition of the hot water system during your inspection, providing insights that help you plan ahead.

Why Hot Water Systems Matter

While not usually top-of-mind during a walk-through, hot water systems matter more than we realize:

- Comfort: No one likes a cold shower.
- Safety: Systems should maintain safe water temperatures and vent properly.

- Efficiency: Older or oversized tanks can waste energy.
- Cost: Aging or undersized systems can drive up your energy bills.

Whether your system is brand-new or hanging on from another era, understanding what you've got and how long it might last is key.

What Clients Should Understand

Hot water systems come in a few different styles, each with its own advantages and quirks:

Tank Water Heaters

- Most common in older homes.
- Store and heat a large volume of water (usually 30–80 gallons).
- Life expectancy: 5–10 years.
- Recovery rate: the time it takes to heat a full tank after use, can be slower in older models, especially if sediment buildup has occurred.

On-Demand (Tankless) Water Heaters

- Heat water only when needed.
- More efficient in homes with lower simultaneous demand.
- Life expectancy: 15–20 years.

- Some models serve dual functions, providing both hot water and radiant heat.
- May struggle with simultaneous high-demand use (e.g., running a shower and laundry at once).

Boiler-Based Hot Water (Tankless Coil Systems)

- Common in older New England homes.
- Uses the home's boiler to heat water directly.
- No dedicated storage tank.
- Efficient in winter when the boiler runs regularly but less efficient in summer.
- Add-on holding tanks improve delivery time and energy use.

Arrow notes whether your system uses a standalone tank, is off the boiler, or is tankless. All are functional solutions, but owners should understand how they operate and what to expect in terms of performance and future replacement.

Venting and Exhaust: What Goes In Must Go Out

Just as important as heating water is safely exhausting the byproducts of combustion. Depending on your system's fuel source and configuration, venting may happen one of two ways:

- Chimney Venting: Common in older systems, especially oil or gas-fueled water heaters. Hot exhaust gases rise through a flue or chimney and exit the home above the roofline. This method requires:

- Proper liner material (metal or clay)
- Clearance from combustibles
- Draft control and maintenance

- Direct Venting: More common in newer systems, especially high-efficiency models. Exhaust gases are forced outside through a PVC or metal pipe, typically through the sill or wall near the unit.
  - Includes intake and exhaust lines (sealed combustion)
  - Safer and more energy-efficient
  - Not dependent on the use of a chimney

Improper venting is a safety concern risking back drafting, carbon monoxide exposure, or poor system performance. Arrow will note venting style, visible defects, and proper termination location during your inspection.

What to Ask Your Inspector

- What type of hot water system is installed?
- How old is the unit, and what is its expected remaining life?
- Are there any signs of corrosion or improper installation?

- Is the system off the boiler, tankless, or a dedicated tank?
- Are safety measures in place, such as TPR (Temperature Pressure Relief) valves or drain lines?

How Arrow Home Inspections Supports You

During the inspection, Arrow will:

- Confirm the type and energy source of the water heater
- Check for visible signs of corrosion, leaks, or faulty installation
- Inspect TPR valves and discharge lines
- Verify safe water temperature and secure installation
- Note any off-boiler or dual-purpose systems

Our goal is to help you understand what's in the home and how to keep it running (or replace it when the time comes).

Frequent Flyers on the Inspection Report

Hot water systems are durable but not immortal.

Common Findings:

- Corrosion or Rust on Tank Exterior: May indicate nearing end of life.
- Improper TPR Valve Discharge Line: Must terminate in a

visible, safe location.

- No Expansion Tank (when required): Necessary on closed systems to manage pressure.
- Incorrect Clearance of Combustibles: Safety issue, especially in enclosed installations.
- Tankless Systems Without Filters or Maintenance Records: Can suffer internal buildup if not regularly flushed.

Final Thought: Heat It When You Need It

Your hot water system isn't flashy, but it's fundamental. You may not think about it every day, but it quietly powers your showers, laundry, and dishes. Whether it's a high-tech tankless setup or a sturdy off-boiler system from decades ago, knowing how it works (and how long it might last) helps you avoid cold surprises and costly emergencies. Like most things in your home, a little knowledge and regular maintenance go a long way.

Hot Water Terms Made Simple

Tank Water Heater: A system that stores and heats water in a tank, usually 30–80 gallons.

On-Demand (Tankless): A compact unit that heats water only when needed. More efficient but may have limited flow.

Tankless Coil: A type of water heater that uses a home's boiler to heat water through a coil, without storage.

Holding Tank: An add-on tank to a tankless coil system that stores heated water for better flow and efficiency.

Recovery Rate: The time it takes a water heater to reheat its full tank after being depleted.

TPR Valve: Temperature Pressure Relief valve. A safety device that releases water if temperature or pressure gets too high.

Expansion Tank: A small tank that absorbs pressure caused by thermal expansion in closed water systems.

Combustion Chamber: The area where fuel is burned to heat water. Must be kept clear of flammable materials.

Scalding Risk: Hot water over 120°F can cause burns. Anti-scald devices or settings can help prevent injury.

Energy Factor (EF): A measure of a water heater's efficiency. Higher numbers mean better performance.

Explore Real-World Inspection Insights

Want to see what our inspectors actually find in the field? Visit our page for real photos and helpful context, organized by the same sections you've just read about. Whether you're buying, selling, or just curious, this gallery gives you a behind-the-scenes look at what we see or how to spot issues before they become problems.

Start exploring at Inspection Insights: arrow-homeinspections.com/inspection-insights or scan the QR code at the end of each chapter.

Heat (AC) and Hot Water

Chapter Fourteen

Plumbing System

What's Flowing Beneath the Surface

THE PLUMBING SYSTEM OF a home may not always be visible, but it's one of the most important functional systems in the house. From freshwater delivery to safe wastewater removal, your plumbing system ensures comfort, cleanliness, and safety.

Arrow Home Inspections evaluates all visible and accessible portions of the plumbing system, including supply lines, waste and vent lines, fixtures, and the location of shut-off valves. While we don't evaluate hidden pipes, we do conduct flow tests to look for signs of corrosion, leakage, outdated materials, and poor installation.

Why Plumbing Systems Matter

Plumbing issues are among the most expensive and disruptive problems a homeowner can face. A leaking pipe or slow drain might seem small but could signal larger concerns like hidden water damage, mold growth, or structural deterioration. Left unchecked, even minor plumbing problems can escalate into costly repairs and health hazards. Water intrusion from faulty pipes can compromise insulation, flooring, and framing—leading to rot, warped materials, or insect infestations. In addition, outdated plumbing materials like galvanized steel or lead can affect both functionality and water quality. That's why a thorough inspection of visible plumbing components is essential for ensuring a home's long-term safety and livability.

Common plumbing-related problems include:

* Water damage and mold

* Poor water pressure or flow

* Aging or failing materials like cast iron or galvanized pipe

* Inefficient or leaky fixtures

* Safety issues with gas lines or shut-off valves

A solid plumbing system supports your daily routines; baths, laundry, cooking, cleaning, and keeps your home safe from water damage and contamination.

What Clients Should Understand

During the inspection, Arrow will run water through sinks, tubs, and showers, flush toilets, and check exposed pipes for leaks or signs of age. Here's what you need to know:

* Water Supply Lines: Typically made of copper, PEX, or older galvanized steel. In some homes, especially older properties, cast iron

may also be present, though it's more commonly used for drain lines. Copper and PEX are durable and standard in modern systems, while galvanized steel and cast iron can corrode over time. *Of special note: Lead Pipes or Solder. Homes built before 1950 may still have lead service lines or lead-based solder joints on copper pipes. Because lead poses serious health risks, Arrow will alert clients to any visible lead components and recommend further testing or replacement based on observations.

* Waste Lines: These remove wastewater and are typically cast iron in older homes or PVC in newer construction. Cracks, rust, and poor connections are red flags.

* Shut-Off Valves: Arrow identifies the location of main shut-offs for water and gas. You should know where these are in case of emergency.

* Functional Flow: We evaluate the water flow at multiple fixtures to see if there's a pressure drop, which could indicate clogs or buildup.

* Drainage: We observe how well water drains and whether drain stops function. Standing water or gurgling sounds may mean poor venting or clogs.

What to Ask Your Inspector

* Are there signs of leaks or corrosion in the visible plumbing?

* What materials are the supply and waste lines made of?

* Are there concerns with water flow or drainage speed?

* Where are the water and gas shut-off valves located?

* Are the drain lines showing signs of age or damage?

How Arrow Home Inspections Supports You

Arrow's goal is to help you understand the condition and functionality of the home's plumbing system by examining:

* Visible water supply and waste piping

* Water flow and drainage at sinks, tubs, and toilets

* Fixture condition and installation

* Exposed lines and potential safety concerns

* Main shut-off valve locations for water and fuel sources

While we don't inspect behind walls or test for water purity, we provide a realistic picture of how the system is working and what might need further evaluation.

Frequent Flyers on the Inspection Report

Many homes, especially older ones, have plumbing quirks. These common findings don't always mean disaster, but they're worth knowing before you buy.

Common Findings:

* Taped or Repaired Drain Lines: Temporary fixes that may need permanent repairs.

* Cast Iron Corrosion: Common in older homes; rust or leaks suggest replacement may be needed soon.

* Oxidized Gas Lines: Not an emergency, but lines should be cleaned and painted to prevent further deterioration.

* Missing Drain Stops or Loose Fixtures: Often a simple fix, but they affect function and resale readiness.

* Poor Functional Flow: Often related to aging pipes or mineral buildup. May require repiping or flushing.

Final Thought: Keep It Flowing

Plumbing should work quietly and reliably in the background. Arrow helps uncover what's flowing properly and what might back up your plans. Even small leaks or slow drains can hint at larger systemic issues, especially in older homes where materials may be near the end of their lifespan. By understanding the current condition of your plumbing system, you can make smart decisions about maintenance, budgeting, and long-term peace of mind.

Plumbing System Terms Made Simple

Supply Line: Pipes that bring fresh water into the home, typically copper or PEX.

Waste Line: Pipes that carry wastewater away from the home, typically cast iron or PVC.

Shut-Off Valve: A manual valve used to stop the water or gas flow in an emergency.

Functional Flow: The consistency of water pressure when multiple fixtures are used.

Drain Stop: A plug or stopper in a sink or tub to block or allow water to drain.

Galvanized Pipe: Steel pipe coated with zinc, used in older homes; prone to corrosion.

PEX: Cross-linked polyethylene tubing used in modern plumbing; flexible and durable.

Cast Iron Pipe: Thick, heavy pipe used in older waste systems; durable but rusts internally.

Oxidation: Rust or corrosion on metal pipes from moisture exposure.

Trap: U-shaped pipe that prevents sewer gases from entering the home.

Vent Stack: A pipe that allows air into the drain system to maintain flow and prevent siphoning.

Fixture: Any device that uses water; faucets, toilets, tubs, or showers.

Explore Real-World Inspection Insights

Want to see what our inspectors actually find in the field? Visit our page for real photos and helpful context, organized by the same sections you've just read about. Whether you're buying, selling, or just curious, this gallery gives you a behind-the-scenes look at what we see or how to spot issues before they become problems.

Start exploring at Inspection Insights: arrow-homeinspections.com/inspection-insights or scan the QR code at the end of each chapter.

Plumbing and Electric

Chapter Fifteen

Electrical System

Power to the People (and the Appliances, and the Lights... and the Panel)

FROM THE SERVICE LINE outside your home to the outlets by your bedside, the electrical system plays a critical role in safety, functionality, and modern convenience. A home inspection includes a visual assessment of accessible electrical components to help identify outdated wiring, overloaded panels, or potential safety hazards.

Arrow Home Inspections evaluates service panels, wiring, receptacles, grounding, and safety devices like GFCIs to ensure your home's electrical system meets modern expectations and points out what doesn't.

Why Electrical Systems Matter

Electrical issues are among the most common causes of house fires and can easily go unnoticed without inspection. Understanding your system's capacity, condition, and configuration is crucial for:

* Safe operation of appliances and fixtures

* Meeting current building codes

* Supporting modern power demands (think: EV chargers, home offices)

* Planning future upgrades or renovations

What Clients Should Understand

* Amperage & Capacity: Most modern homes require at least 100 amps. Many older homes were built with 60-amp service, which is insufficient for today's needs.

* Panel Type: Homes today use circuit breakers, not fuses. Fuses are often outdated and a red flag for some clients and insurers.

* Wiring Types: Older homes may include knob and tube, BX cable, or a mix of types. Newer homes use Romex (NM) cable.

* Grounding: Grounding rods and wires reduce electrocution risk and protect devices. An ungrounded system may require upgrades.

* Aluminum Wiring: Common in the 1960s and 70s, it expands/contrasts more than copper and can pose a fire risk if not properly maintained.

Special Note: Solar Panels

If a home has solar panels, the system itself is typically outside the scope of a general inspection. However, Arrow will report if:

* Panels appear damaged or improperly mounted

* The electrical panel includes breakers or subpanels related to solar generation

* There are signs of back-feeding (also known as grid back-feeding) or improper labeling

Licensed electricians and solar professionals should evaluate system performance and code compliance.

Historic Home Wiring: Knob, Tube, and Beyond

Homes built before 1920 may contain knob and tube wiring; a system of ceramic knobs and open-air wiring that lacks grounding. While it may still function, it's considered outdated and potentially dangerous. Insurance companies often refuse to insure homes with active knob and tube wiring.

Other early systems include BX cable, a metal-sheathed wire common before the 1960s. Unlike today's Romex, BX often lacks a separate ground wire and may deteriorate with age.

What to Ask Your Inspector

* What is the home's amperage and service capacity?

* Are there any signs of outdated or unsafe wiring (e.g., knob and tube)?

* Is the panel at or near capacity?

* Are all outlets properly grounded and GFCI-protected where required?

* Is the main service line secured and weather-tight?

How Arrow Home Inspections Supports You

Arrow Home Inspection, in some states doesn't remove panel covers or inspect behind walls, but we do evaluate visible components such as:

* Main panel type, size, and capacity

* Presence and function of GFCI outlets and breakers

* Visible wiring types and condition

* Service line entrance, drip loop, and sealant

* Grounding wires and bonding connections

In states requiring multiple experts to inspect aspects of the home, Arrow relies on its trusted network of industry experts to attend your home inspection and provide you with the information you need to feel confident about your elect panel and beyond.

Pro Tip: One of the most overlooked and easily corrected issues? Missing or deteriorated electrical putty at the service entrance. This small fix can prevent water from entering the panel and causing serious problems.

Frequent Flyers on the Inspection Report

Many electrical concerns are inexpensive to correct but important to address. These findings show up often on inspection reports:

* Missing Knockout Covers: Exposes interior of panel—easy fix, but safety issue.

* Overloaded Panels: When all breaker slots are full, mini-breakers or tandem breakers may be improperly used.

* Loose or Ungrounded Outlets: Especially in older homes or DIY renovations.

* Improper Drip Loops: Drip loops help keep rainwater from following the wire into the panel. Missing or poorly configured loops are common.

* Lack of GFCI/AFCI Protection: Modern code requires these outlets in kitchens, baths, garages, and exteriors.

Final Thought: Shocking How Much You Didn't Know

Electricity runs everything, until it doesn't. From your fridge to your furnace, the electric system is the silent force keeping your home functional and your family safe. But outdated wiring, overloaded panels, or something as simple as a missing drip loop or deteriorated putty can create real hazards.

A home's electrical system isn't just about power, it's about protection. Making sure everything is grounded, sealed, and supported by the right capacity can prevent costly damage, reduce fire risk, and even save lives. Don't overlook the basics or assume "if it works, it's fine." Safety starts at the panel and continues with every switch, outlet, and connection.

Electrical System Terms Made Simple

Breaker Panel: A modern electrical panel that protects circuits by tripping when overloaded.

Fuse Panel: An older type of electrical panel that uses fuses instead of breakers. Often considered outdated.

Romex (NM) Cable: A modern type of plastic-sheathed electrical wiring used in homes today.

BX Cable: Early metal-armored electrical cable. Durable, but may lack grounding.

Knob and Tube Wiring: A very old system of open-air wires mounted on ceramic knobs. Not grounded, often uninsurable.

Drip Loop: A downward bend in the overhead service line that prevents rain from entering the electrical box.

Candy Cane Conduit: A curved metal pipe often used to carry wires above the roofline for overhead electrical entry.

GFCI Outlet: Ground Fault Circuit Interrupter—shuts off power when a ground fault is detected.

AFCI Outlet: Arc Fault Circuit Interrupter—protects against fire caused by electrical arcing.

Grounding Rod: A metal rod driven into the earth to safely discharge electrical current from the system.

Service Entrance Cable: The wire that runs from the utility to your main panel.

Putty Seal: Weatherproof sealant around the electrical service entry to keep out moisture.

Solar Backfeed: When solar panels send unused electricity back to the power grid (requires proper labeling/setup).

Explore Real-World Inspection Insights

Want to see what our inspectors actually find in the field? Visit our page for real photos and helpful context, organized by the same sections you've just read about. Whether you're buying, selling, or just curious, this gallery gives you a behind-the-scenes look at what we see or how to spot issues before they become problems.

Start exploring at Inspection Insights: arrow-homeinspections.com/inspection-insights or scan the QR code at the end of each chapter.

Plumbing and Electric

Chapter Sixteen

Asbestos

What You Need to Know

It Shows Up Where You Least Expect It

Asbestos is one of those topics that can come up in any part of a home inspection from the basement to the attic and everywhere in between. Because it can appear in so many forms and locations, it's important to understand the basics of what asbestos is, where it might be found, and what your next steps should be if it's suspected. Rather than repeat this information across several chapters, we've dedicated this section to addressing it clearly and thoroughly.

Why Asbestos Matters

Asbestos is a naturally occurring mineral once prized for its fire resistance, insulation properties, and durability. It was widely used in homes built before the mid-1980s, however its use continued into the early 1990's. However, it's now known to pose serious health risks particularly when it becomes airborne and is inhaled. Asbestos exposure has been linked to lung cancer, mesothelioma, and other respiratory diseases.

While intact asbestos is often best left undisturbed, damaged or deteriorating materials may require professional testing, abatement, or encapsulation.

Common Residential Materials That May Contain Asbestos

In Massachusetts, Rhode Island, and Connecticut, home inspectors are not licensed to confirm the presence of asbestos, but they are trained to identify materials that are suspect based on age and appearance. Here are areas where asbestos may commonly be found:

- Vinyl Floor Tiles (often 9x9, 12x12, or 6x6) or linoleum
- Ceiling Tiles (12 x 12) common in main living spaces
- Adhesive or mastic under flooring
- Boiler and heating pipe wrap (typically white cloth-like or crumbly material)
- Popcorn or textured ceilings
- Roofing shingles or siding shingles (especially cement board siding)
- Asbestos-containing insulation (like vermiculite in attics)
- Transite pipes in older plumbing systems
- Plaster and drywall joint compounds (in some pre-1980s

homes)

- Exterior siding shingles

What to Ask Your Inspector

Because inspectors can't legally test for asbestos without appropriate licensure, your best course of action is to ask:

- Are there any materials in the home that may contain asbestos?
- What is the condition of these materials? Are they intact, crumbling, or disturbed?
- Do you recommend having a licensed asbestos inspector or abatement contractor evaluate specific areas?

What Arrow Home Inspections Looks For

Arrow will not confirm asbestos but will flag areas of concern and clearly label them as "Asbestos-like materials" or "Potential ACMs (Asbestos-Containing Materials)" in the report. Our inspectors evaluate:

- Age of the property and known risk periods (typically pre-1980s construction)
- Visible signs of damage or deterioration in suspect materials
- Unusual or older-looking insulation, flooring, ceiling tex-

ture, or siding

- Pipe wrap and basement materials that match common asbestos patterns

What You Should Do

If suspect asbestos materials are found:

- Do not disturb them: Drilling, sanding, cutting, or removing them can release dangerous fibers.
- Keep an eye on condition: If intact and undisturbed, many asbestos materials can remain in place or encapsulated.
- Hire a licensed asbestos professional for testing and, if needed, abatement or encapsulation.
- In Massachusetts, Rhode Island, and Connecticut, only licensed asbestos inspectors and abatement contractors can legally test and remove ACMs.

Frequent Flyers on the Inspection Report

- Old Pipe Wrap in the Basement: Common in homes built before 1980. Often friable and damaged.
- 9x9 Floor Tiles – Almost always flagged as suspect. Frequently found in basements and kitchens.
- Vermiculite Insulation – Particularly the Zonolite brand,

which has been linked to asbestos contamination.

- Siding Shingles – Especially grayish, cement-like siding used in mid-century homes.

Final Thought: Respect It, Don't Panic

Asbestos doesn't mean a house is unsafe—it means you need a plan. Arrow Home Inspections helps you recognize potential risks without jumping to conclusions. In many cases, materials can be managed with monitoring or professional sealing. Our goal is to make sure you understand what you're seeing, what it means, and who to call if you need help.

Asbestos Glossary

ACM (Asbestos-Containing Material): Any material suspected or confirmed to contain asbestos. Must be tested by a licensed pro.

Friable: A material that crumbles easily when touched, increasing risk of airborne fibers.

Encapsulation: A process where asbestos material is coated with a sealant to prevent fiber release.

Vermiculite: A type of attic insulation that may contain asbestos, especially if from Zonolite.

Pipe Wrap: Cloth-like material once used for insulating heating pipes; often contains asbestos.

Popcorn Ceiling: Textured ceiling finish popular in older homes, may contain asbestos if installed before 1980.

Chapter Seventeen

Inspection Types & Add-On Services

The Basics and Beyond

A STANDARD HOME INSPECTION is just the beginning. At Arrow Home Inspections, we understand that every property and every client has unique needs. That's why we offer a range of inspection types and add-on services designed to give you as much (or as little) information as you need, all in a clear, actionable format.

Whether you're purchasing a manufactured home, walking through an open house, or need a re-check after repairs, Arrow helps you get straight to the point with the right service for the situation.

Core Inspection Types

Standard Home Inspection
Our most requested service, this comprehensive inspection evaluates the visible and accessible systems and components of a home. It includes structural elements, roofing, HVAC, plumbing, electrical sys-

tems, insulation, ventilation, interior elements, and appliances. Ideal for buyers under contract or sellers preparing to list their home (See chapter 20 for specific seller information).

Manufactured Home Inspection

Tailored to factory-built or mobile homes, this inspection addresses the unique materials and construction methods used in these properties. We look at the chassis, piers, tie-downs, skirting, and utilities, identifying signs of improper installation, movement, or deferred maintenance. A must-have for buyers or current owners wanting peace of mind.

Limited Element Inspection

This focused inspection assesses a specific area of concern like the roof, foundation, HVAC system, or plumbing without evaluating the whole house. It's perfect for investors, landlords, or current owners needing quick answers before scheduling a full repair.

Walk-and-Talk

Not under contract yet? We'll meet you at a private showing and walk the property together. No formal report, just our honest insights, experience-based feedback, and a conversation about what you're seeing and what to look for. Great for buyers wanting to make informed offers without committing to a full inspection.

Re-Inspection

After seller repairs are made, this service verifies that the work was completed as agreed. We re-evaluate only the previously flagged items, ensuring they were corrected properly and safely. Re-inspections help avoid surprises before closing.

Add-On Services

Radon Testing

Radon is a naturally occurring, odorless gas that can accumulate in homes and is thought to be a leading cause of lung cancer. We place specialized equipment in the lowest livable level of the home for a minimum of 48 hours, then retrieve and interpret the results. Early testing can prevent long-term health risks.

Water Quality Testing

For homes with private wells or even just for peace of mind. Water testing checks for contaminants like bacteria, lead, nitrates, and more. We collect a sample and deliver it to a certified lab. This is especially important for homes with children or vulnerable residents.

Septic Inspection Coordination

If a property has a septic system, it needs its own specialist. We coordinate with a licensed septic inspector to evaluate tank integrity, baffle condition, sludge levels, and leach field function. Catching septic issues early can save thousands.

Pest Inspection Coordination

Worried about termites, carpenter ants, or other wood-destroying insects? We'll schedule a pest control professional to inspect for signs of activity or damage, often during the same window as the home inspection for maximum convenience.

Sewer Scope (Main Drain Camera)

This inspection uses a camera to examine the main sewer line from the house to the street. We're looking for blockages, root intrusion, cracks, or sagging in the line. It's especially useful for older homes or any home with slow drains or past issues.

Mold or Air Quality Testing

If musty smells or staining are present, or if a family member has allergies, mold or indoor air testing can help identify hidden issues. We collect samples to evaluate moisture intrusion and potential mold spore levels.

Why Add-On Services Matter

A standard inspection looks at the big picture but sometimes you need a closer lens. Add-on services provide added insight into the systems that could impact your health, safety, or unexpected future costs. Bundling them with your inspection saves time and often catches concerns before they become problems.

Final Thought: Choose Your Path to Peace of Mind

No two homes and no two clients are the same. Whether you want a deep dive into the drains or just a quick once-over before you offer, Arrow Home Inspections offers a solution that fits. We're here to support you with straight talk, smart services, and clear choices at every step of the journey.

Chapter Eighteen

Radon

What You Can't See Can Hurt You

When it comes to protecting your home and health, one of the most overlooked threats is also one of the most silent: radon gas. Odorless, colorless, and tasteless, radon can seep into your home without warning and the only way to know it's there is to test for it.

What Is Radon?

Radon is a naturally occurring radioactive gas formed when uranium breaks down in soil, rock, and groundwater. It exists all around us in the environment, but it becomes a concern when it enters and accumulates in enclosed spaces like the basement or lower levels of your home.

Why Is Radon Dangerous?

According to the U.S. Environmental Protection Agency (EPA), radon is the second leading cause of lung cancer in the United States, right behind smoking. (https://www.epa.gov/radon/are-we-sure-radon-health-risk?) In fact, long-term exposure to elevated radon levels can pose a serious health risk, even in non-smokers. Because it's invisible and doesn't cause immediate symptoms, many homeowners are unaware of their exposure until it's too late.

How Does Radon Get into a Home?

Radon gas moves up from the ground and can enter your home through cracks in the foundation, gaps in floors or walls, around service pipes, or even through well water. Homes with basements or crawlspaces tend to have the highest radon levels, but any home, in any area, can be affected including new builds and homes without visible foundation issues.

Why Testing Matters; Now and Later

Most homebuyers know to test for radon during the purchase process. But what many don't realize is that radon levels can change over time. Shifting soils, renovations, changes in heating or ventilation, or even nearby construction can alter airflow and pressure, affecting how much radon enters the home. That's why ongoing testing is just as important as initial testing.

At Arrow Home Inspections, we use calibrated, continuous monitoring devices to provide accurate radon test results during the home inspection process. These devices track radon levels over a 48-hour period, showing any fluctuations and giving a true picture of potential risk.

Why It Matters for Buyers, Sellers, and Agents

- **Buyers**: A radon test can help you make an informed decision before purchasing. Knowing if mitigation is needed can influence negotiations or budgeting for future safety improvements.
- **Sellers**: A pre-listing radon test shows buyers that you've taken your role seriously and addressed potential concerns upfront. It can add confidence and transparency to the sale.
- **Agents**: Radon testing helps reduce liability and builds trust. Encouraging clients to test for radon demonstrates professionalism and concern for long-term safety, not just closing the deal.

Final Thought: Protect What Matters Most

Radon may be invisible, but its risks are very real. The good news? It's detectable and fixable. Regular testing gives you peace of mind and helps protect your home's value and your family's health.

The information here is based on current guidance from the EPA and leading home safety organizations. However, always consult a licensed radon professional for mitigation or questions about test results. Arrow Home Inspections is here to help whether you're buying, selling, or simply want to make sure your home stays a safe place to live.

Chapter Nineteen

Sewer Scope Inspections

What Lies Beneath

Why Sewer Scans Matter; Even When Everything *Seems* Fine

When you picture a home inspection, you probably think about the roof, the plumbing, or maybe the foundation. But one of the most expensive and often overlooked systems in a home is the one you can't see at all: the sewer line.

A sewer scope inspection (or sewer scan) involves running a specialized camera through the main waste line that carries wastewater from the home to the municipal sewer or private septic system. It may sound like a specialty service, but it's becoming a standard recommendation—especially for older homes, homes with large trees nearby, or any property where the sewer line's condition is unknown.

What Can Go Wrong?

Sewer lines are typically made of cast iron, clay, ABS plastic, or PVC. Each has its own lifespan and vulnerabilities. Over time, these pipes can crack, corrode, shift, or get blocked; leading to backups, bad odors, or even catastrophic failure. Common issues include:

- **Tree root intrusion**, which can crack or clog the pipe
- **Bellies or sags** where waste and water collect, leading to backups
- **Offset or collapsed joints** from soil shifting or poor installation
- **Grease buildup**, foreign objects, or blockages from previous use
- **Deterioration in older materials**, like Orangeburg or clay pipe

Many of these issues aren't visible during a standard inspection and may not cause symptoms right away until they do. That's why a proactive scan can be a game changer.

Who Should Consider a Sewer Scope?

While sewer scopes are especially recommended for:

- Homes older than 30 years
- Homes with mature trees near the sewer path
- Properties with slow drains or previous backup history
- Any home where no prior scan has been documented

...they're also a wise choice for cautious buyers of newer construction. Even brand-new homes can have improperly sloped lines, construction debris, or misaligned joints that could cause problems down the line.

What Happens During a Scan?

At Arrow Home Inspections, we use a high-resolution, calibrated camera to inspect the line from an accessible cleanout or drain. We record the findings, take still shots of any issues, and provide a clear, easy-to-understand summary. If a problem is found, we'll let you know whether it's cosmetic, urgent, or simply something to monitor and recommend next steps accordingly.

Ongoing Maintenance & Awareness

Just like radon or roof wear, sewer issues can develop slowly and quietly. That's why it's a good idea to **test periodically,** especially if you experience gurgling drains, slow flushing toilets, or foul smells.

Preventive scanning is an investment in peace of mind and can save you from unexpected repairs that often range from $5,000 to $25,000 depending on the issue.

Final Thought: Don't Let Problems Back Up on You

Your home's sewer system works behind the scenes but when something goes wrong, it moves front and center quickly. A sewer scan gives you the chance to spot issues before they become emergencies.

Whether you're buying a home or want to stay ahead of costly surprises in the one you already own, this is one step you won't regret.

Have questions or need to schedule a scan? Arrow Home Inspections is here to help, offering reliable insight and referrals if more specialized work is needed. As always, this information is intended to be educational. For guidance specific to your property, contact Arrow Home Inspections for a sewer scan today!

Chapter Twenty

Sellers, Get Ahead of the Market

Inspections That Put Sellers in Control

LISTING YOUR HOME IS a big move emotionally, financially, and logistically. One of the best tools a seller can have isn't just a fresh coat of paint or staging furniture, it's knowledge. Knowing the condition of your property before the buyer makes an offer or sends in their inspector can be the difference between closing with confidence or scrambling during negotiations.

At Arrow Home Inspections, we help sellers see their homes through a buyer's eyes before the home ever hits the market.

Why Sellers Should Consider a Pre-Listing Inspection

Most sellers wait for the buyer's inspection report to learn about issues that may affect the sale. But that reactive approach can backfire. A pre-listing inspection allows you to:

- Identify and repair issues before buyers do

- Avoid last-minute surprises or renegotiations
- Price your home more confidently
- Provide a report to build buyer trust
- Reduce the risk of deals falling apart due to inspection findings

Buyers appreciate transparency and being the seller who's already done the homework makes your property stand out.

What Arrow Offers Sellers

Pre-Listing Inspection

This comprehensive inspection looks at all major systems and visible components of the home—roof, foundation, heating, plumbing, electrical, and more. You'll receive a full report with photos and easy-to-understand findings that give you a realistic picture of your home's condition.

You can choose to address major concerns before listing—or simply disclose them and price the property accordingly. Either way, you're steering the ship.

Walk-and-Talk for Sellers

Not ready for a full report? No problem. We offer a walk-and-talk consultation designed specifically for sellers. This informal service includes a guided walkthrough with one of our inspectors, providing on-the-spot insights and observations. No formal report is delivered—just clear, candid advice about what might come up in a buyer's inspection.

Ideal for sellers who:

- Want a second opinion before listing
- Plan to sell "as-is" but want to know what to expect
- Don't want to over-improve or spend unnecessarily

Optional Add-On Services for Sellers

Selling a home with well water or a septic system? Concerned about pests or radon? Arrow can arrange for any ancillary services you may want to get ahead of before your buyer does.

Available services include:

- Radon Testing
- Water Quality Testing
- Sewer Line Camera Scope
- Pest Inspection Coordination
- Septic Inspection Coordination
- Mold/Air Quality Testing

Bundling these with your pre-listing inspection ensures you know *everything* before anyone else does.

Control the Narrative

One of the most powerful benefits of a pre-listing inspection is being able to address findings *on your terms*. You can:

- Hire contractors you trust
- Disclose known issues upfront
- Prevent buyers from inflating the cost of repairs during negotiations
- Use your report as a transparency tool in marketing your home

When you hand the buyer a clean report or a report with disclosed issues already reflected in the list price you build trust, reduce stress, and often shorten the time on market.

How Arrow Supports Sellers

Whether you want a quick walk-through or a full detailed inspection, Arrow tailors services to your timeline and goals. Our inspectors are trained to speak in plain language and provide context for each finding so you don't just know *what* needs attention, but *why* and *how much it matters*.

We'll also help you determine which items are minor, which are cosmetic, and which may be worth fixing before you go to market.

Frequent Flyers for Sellers

These are the items that often surprise sellers, especially in older homes but show up regularly on buyer inspection reports.

Common Findings:

- Leaking Fixtures or Slow Drains: Easy fixes that can look like bigger problems.
- Loose Railings or Steps: Simple safety items buyers love to see resolved.
- Roof Aging or Minor Damage: Get an honest look at the roof's condition now—before a buyer brings in a roofer.
- Outlet or GFCI Issues: Low-cost fixes that buyers love to nitpick.
- Water Stains or Settling Cracks: May be cosmetic, but buyers want reassurance. Get it documented.

Final Thought: You Can't Fix What You Don't Know

Selling your home is about putting your best foot forward and nothing helps you do that better than knowing where you stand. With a pre-listing inspection or seller's walk-through, Arrow Home Inspections helps you prepare, present, and protect your property like a pro.

Buyers love informed sellers. Your future self at the closing table will thank you.

Book an Inspection

Looking for more information on Doug Cavalieri or Arrow Home Inspections?

Visit Arrow-HomeInspections.com

Ready to book an inspection?

Visit **StraightToThePointWithArrow.com**

Made in the USA
Middletown, DE
24 September 2025

17464852R00104